DOLCI *Italiani*

DOLCI *Italiani*

DESSERTS, CAKES & OTHER SWEET BAKES FROM ITALY

Ursula Ferrigno

photography by **CLARE WINFIELD**

RYLAND PETERS & SMALL

DEDICATION

*To Mummy and Daddy
in their memory.*

Senior Designer Toni Kay
Senior Editor Abi Waters
Head of Production
  Patricia Harrington
Creative Director
  Leslie Harrington
Editorial Director Julia Charles

Food Stylist Kathy Kordalis
Prop Stylist Zoe Harrington
Indexer Vanessa Bird

First published in 2025 by
Ryland Peters & Small
20–21 Jockey's Fields, London
WC1R 4BW
and
1452 Davis Bugg Road
Warrenton, NC 27589

www.rylandpeters.com
email: euregulations@rylandpeters.com

10 9 8 7 6 5 4 3 2 1

Text © Ursula Ferrigno 2025
Design and commissioned photography
© Ryland Peters & Small 2025

Printed in China.

ISBN: 978-1-78879-682-8

A CIP record for this book is available
from the British Library.
US Library of Congress cataloging-in-
Publication Data has been applied for.

The authorised representative
in the EEA is
Authorised Rep Compliance Ltd.,
Ground Floor, 71 Lower Baggot Street,
Dublin, D02 P593, Ireland
www.arccompliance.com

NOTES

• All spoon measurements are level
unless otherwise specified.
• All eggs are medium (UK) or large (US),
unless specified as large, in which case
US extra-large should be used. Uncooked
or partially cooked eggs should not
be served to the very old, frail, young
children, pregnant women or those
with compromised immune systems.
• When a recipe calls for cling film/
plastic wrap, you can substitute for
beeswax wraps, silicone stretch lids
or compostable baking paper for
greater sustainability.
• When a recipe calls for the grated
zest of citrus fruit, buy unwaxed fruit
and wash well before using.
• Ovens should be preheated to the
specified temperatures.

CONTENTS

Introduction 6

CAKES 10
Torte

TARTS & SWEET BREADS 48
Crostate e pani dolci

SMALL CAKES, PASTRIES & BISCUITS 86
Pasticcini e biscotti

DESSERTS 116
Dolci

ICE CREAM & SORBETS 136
Gelati, semifreddi e sorbetti

EDIBLE GIFTS 152
Regali 151

Index 174
Acknowledgements 176

INTRODUCTION

The Italians, as a nation, have a very sweet tooth, and sweet things are very much part of daily life. This passion is said to have been inspired by the seafaring and trading Venetians, who were among the first in Europe to refine and trade in sugar. Up until about the 12th century, honey and fruit were the only sweeteners in the West (plus maple syrup in North America). It is not clear who first discovered the properties of sugar cane, but the Arabs certainly knew how to refine it, and this ensuing 'white gold' was introduced to Europe, via soldiers returning from the 11th-century Crusades. The Venetians then developed sugar-refining factories in Tyre, in modern-day Lebanon, before moving them to the island of Cyprus, a Venetian possession for a time.

The Venetian Republic had a monopoly on sugar (and on spices, coffee and chocolate) until the discovery of America. On his second voyage in 1493, Christopher Columbus planted sugar canes on islands in the Caribbean. There the canes thrived, liking the climate much more than that of Europe, and so the Venetian monopoly was broken. By the 18th century, the West Indian islands were the main world source of sugar, and its production, sadly, contributed massively to the abhorrent slave trade.

The Arabs were also important in other sweet aspects of Italian cuisine. They ruled Sicily for roughly 200 years. Apart from sugar, they introduced many trees, fruits and nuts – chiefly pistachios, figs and citrus fruit – and these are hugely important in many Italian cakes, pastries, biscuits/cookies and puddings. They were also responsible for the ice creams for which Italy is now so renowned. The story goes that they flavoured snow from Mount Etna with fruit juices and syrups, thus inventing *gelati* and *sorbetti*. My recipes in the relevant chapter are a little more sophisticated...

So a liking for sweet flavours has long existed in the Italian palate. And that, married with the Italians' love of celebrating, means that sweet things – cakes, pastries, biscuits – are intuitively associated with occasions such as birthdays, christenings, weddings, saints' days and religious festivals such as Christmas and Easter. But it actually goes further than that: the Italians love sweet things so much that they indulge almost on a daily basis – a quick small pastry with a coffee for breakfast, or a slice of something delicious mid-morning or -afternoon. After the *riposo* (the Italian siesta) is a popular time for having something sweet: this gives a burst of energy for the rest of the day (so they say!). Visiting friends and family conjures up yet another excuse: I wouldn't dream of popping in to see neighbours or friends without taking with me a box or bag of homemade biscuits.

And of course the displays in Italian *pasticcerie* are always so enticing, it is difficult to pass without staring and indulging! In October last year, when I finished teaching in Puglia, some students and I shared some *pasticciotti* (a speciality of the region, see page 103) in a tiny bakery in Specchia: a coffee, pastry and glass of iced water, all served with such pride. I am proud of all the following recipes and hope that some, or many, of them will inspire you.

A FEW NOTES ON INGREDIENTS

To make Italian cakes, pastries, biscuits/cookies and puddings, all you need are good ingredients, and I cannot emphasize this enough. The eggs must be fresh, because the fresher they are, the more air they will trap when beaten, particularly important in sponge-making. Fresh eggs also add colour and inimitable flavour, and I try to find Italian eggs, but you can use free-range or organic. When I use Italian eggs, my pasta is richer and yellower, as are my custards.

The sugar must be caster or superfine; as it is finer than granulated, it blends in more easily. The flour for cakes, sponges and pastries should be plain/all-purpose, soft and sifted (this traps the all-important air): Italian 00 flour is perfect, because it has already been sifted twice (thus the two 0s). I don't, however, use self-raising/rising flour very often, as I think a combination of 00 and baking powder is much more potent. Other flours can also be used, such as buckwheat or chestnut flour, or fine polenta/cornmeal. And please, always, seal a flour packet tightly; it goes stale if exposed to air, which can affect baking results, and can pick up migrating flavours.

Try to buy nuts in the shell, and crack open when needed. They will be much fresher. Fruit should be as fresh as possible, and in good condition. One fruit that I use a lot is the lemon. You can buy unwaxed lemons, but if you are unsure, simply scrub the lemon skin with a clean, soap-free brush under cool running water. Dry before use.

A FEW NOTES ON EQUIPMENT

For most of the recipes in this book, you need an oven, and this should be reliable. If your oven is performing a few degrees of heat up or down from the displayed temperature, this is enough to potentially ruin a cake. To test how efficiently your oven is working, buy an oven thermometer and hang it from the middle rack of the oven. Turn the oven on to about 200°C/Fan 180°C/400°F/Gas 6. Keep the oven door closed until the oven alerts you that it has reached the set temperature. Check the oven thermometer. If the temperatures match, you are fine. If not, perhaps you should get an engineer to have a look.

Other factors come into play when baking in your oven. You must always preheat it before cooking, about 15 minutes usually, and position the shelves carefully. A cake should be in the centre of the oven. And when baking more than one cake at a time, stagger them rather than having them directly above or below each other. Even though your oven might be working well, it is always a good idea, halfway through baking, to turn a cake pan, baking sheet or muffin tray around. But never open the oven door until the item you are cooking has set and is lightly browned or it may sink.

Considering oven pans, you should always use a cake pan the same size as I have specified, otherwise the recipe might not work so well. Similarly, springform pans are better in some circumstances than loose-bottomed. I use middle-weight metal pans, many of them non-stick, which makes cake removal much easier. I use baking paper (also known as greaseproof/wax paper) to line baking sheets and cake pans. I give instructions on how to line cake pans below, but various shapes and forms are available ready-made, as paper liners or silicone moulds, ready-to-use, from good kitchen shops.

LINING ROUND CAKE PANS

1 *Place a sheet of baking paper on your work surface. Cut a strip about 5 cm/2 inches taller than the height of the pan, making sure it is long enough to wrap around the inside of the pan.*

2 *Fold over one long edge of strip by roughly 3 cm/ 1¼ inches. Make a series of small cuts along this folded edge.*

3 *Take another sheet of baking paper and draw a circle around base of the pan. Cut out the circle.*

4 *Lightly grease the bottom and sides of the pan with butter. Press the strip around the sides of the pan with the cut edge folded into the centre of the base. Lay the paper circle in the bottom of the pan over the cut edge.*

LINING LOAF & SQUARE PANS

1 *Grease your pan, then place it on top of a sheet of baking paper. This must be big enough to come up the sides of the pan. Make a pencil mark at each corner of the tin, then cut the paper from the outside diagonally towards the mark at each of the four corners.*

2 *Carefully place the baking paper inside the pan, and the cut edges will overlap, lining the pan snugly. Cut off any excess paper.*

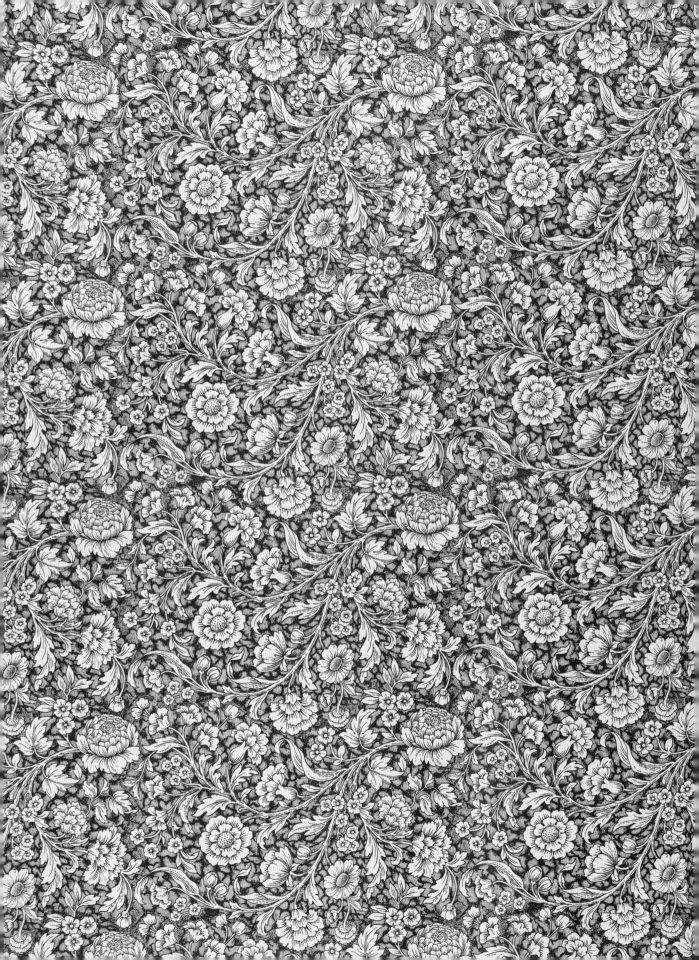

CAKES
Torte

Cakes for every occasion

Italian cakes are luscious and full of flavour, and are made mainly in special pastry shops – *pasticcerie* – rather than in restaurants or at home. Sadly, away from Italy, we don't have easy access to authentic *pasticcerie*, so I am here providing you with recipes for a wonderful array of Italian cakes to make in your own kitchen. They are as delicious as anything shop-bought, probably more so (if I say so myself), and are easy to make.

Most Italian families buy cakes for special occasions such as Easter, Christmas, other Christian celebratory days and for birthdays. But they also eat cake on a day-to-day basis (the Italians really like cake!): with coffee in the morning, for *merenda* (snack) at tea time, or after a meal. I have seen people in cafés having a glass of something alcoholic and a slice of cake for breakfast. I think I draw the line at that...

But one cake is often made at home, and that is the Italian sponge, *pan di Spagna* (so-called because it was introduced to Italy by the Spanish invaders of Sicily). Classically it is a mix of egg yolks and caster/superfine sugar, into which beaten egg whites and flour are gradually folded. The French *savoie* biscuits (the sponge fingers used in tiramisù) and cake are similar. But an Italian sponge cake can also be made using whole eggs, which is similar to the French genoise – the name coming obviously from 'Genoese', suggesting an Italian influence. I wonder which came first? Sometimes butter can be included, which makes the cake denser and slightly longer-lasting. Light, soft and airy, the Genoese sponge cake on page 47 can be

eaten filled or topped, and is used as the basis of many Italian puddings such as *zuppa Inglese* (see page 129), *cassata* (see page 122) or *zuccotto* (see page 126).

Chocolate is a favourite cake flavouring in Italy, as is coffee. Spices make their appearance too, as do many nuts, such as walnuts and hazelnuts. Almonds are even more common, as they grow prolifically in the south, introduced by the Arabs when they ruled Sicily. The Arabs also imported pistachios from the Middle East, and these are used a lot in Italian cake-, biscuit- and gelato-making. I have a real soft spot for pistachios. I love eating them dried and salted, splitting the shells open with my fingernails; they are wonderful cracked and glued decoratively to the sides and top of a creamy cake, and in the ricotta filling of Sicilian cannoli (deep-fried pastry tubes, see page 96).

There is a great Italian tradition of preserving fruit, and these products find their way into many an Italian cake. Some are dried – grapes as raisins, plums as prunes, apricots as themselves! – and eaten as they are, as a wholesome snack or included in cakes and other foods. Some fruits are candied (see page 170), usually the peel of oranges, lemons, grapefruit and citrons. Candied citrus peel is used in the Milanese panettone, in a filling for Sicilian cannoli, and in *cassata*. Candied pumpkin is often used in the classic Tuscan panforte, and chestnuts are candied for the luxurious Italian version of the French *marrons glacés*, *marroni canditi*. (An unusual variation on the theme is *mostarda di Cremona*, where candied fruits is cooked in a mustard syrup and served as an accompaniment to boiled meats or cheese.) But fresh fruits are used too, such as apples, apricots, raspberries and pears, and citrus juices are a common flavouring in cakes from southern Italy. Even vegetables are used: I have given you an unusual Italian carrot cake here!

CHERRY & RICOTTA CAKE
Torta ricotta e ciliegie

Ricotta gives a gloriously squidgy texture to this cake, which is to be enjoyed in the cherry season. We are exposed to many different varietals in Italy, but on a recent trip, we used plums (the same quantity), quartered, in place of cherries to great effect.

150 g/²/₃ cup/1¼ sticks unsalted butter, softened

225 g/1 cup plus 2 tablespoons caster/superfine sugar

250 g/generous 1 cup ricotta

2 lemons, grated zest of both and juice of 1

4 large/US extra-large eggs

1 teaspoon vanilla extract

2 tablespoons cherry vermouth

175 g/1⅓ cups self-raising/ rising flour

½ teaspoon baking powder

½ teaspoon fine sea salt

50 g/½ cup flaked almonds

200 g/1 cup stoned/pitted cherries

icing/confectioners' sugar, for dusting

20-cm/8-inch springform cake pan, greased and lined

Serves 8–10

Preheat the oven to 180°C/160°C fan/350°F/Gas 4.

In a stand mixer, beat the butter and sugar until pale and creamy. Beat in the ricotta and lemon zest until combined. Add the eggs, one at a time, making sure each one is incorporated before adding the next. Beat in the lemon juice, vanilla and cherry vermouth.

Combine the flour, baking powder and salt in a sieve, then sift over the butter mixture and fold together. Fold in half of the almonds until just incorporated, making sure not to over-mix. Scrape the batter into the prepared pan and scatter the cherries on top, followed by the remaining almonds.

Bake in the preheated oven for 50–60 minutes until a skewer inserted comes out clean. Cover with foil towards the end of the cooking time if the cake is browning too much.

Remove from the oven and leave to cool completely in the pan. Release from the pan and lightly dust with icing sugar to serve.

HAZELNUT & CARROT CAKE
Torta di carote e nocciole

This is a winning combination created by my friend Madalena in Selci Lama, a small village near Perugia. If I didn't include this recipe I would be extremely disappointed in myself. She owns a bakery, hence the inclusion of cake crumbs. Most carrot cakes have a cream cheese topping, but the Italian version is just as it is and I find that equally as delicious. A lighter and healthier version.

340 g/12 oz. organic carrots, peeled and finely grated
170 g/1⅓ cups hazelnuts, toasted and ground
60 g/2 oz. cake crumbs (Madeira or sponge cake)
1 teaspoon baking powder
2 teaspoons ground cinnamon
grated zest of 1 lemon

5 large/US extra-large eggs, separated
110 g/½ cup plus 2 teaspoons caster/superfine sugar
icing/confectioners' sugar, for dusting (optional)

23-cm/9-inch cake pan, greased and lined

Serves 6–8

Preheat the oven to 160°C/140°C fan/325°F/Gas 3.

Place the carrots in a bowl with the hazelnuts, cake crumbs, baking powder, cinnamon and lemon zest.

Beat the egg yolks with half the sugar using a stand mixer until thick enough that the whisk will leave a trail. Fold it into the carrot mixture.

Whisk the egg whites until stiff, but not too dry. Whisk in the remaining sugar. Carefully fold the meringue into the carrot mixture using a large metal spoon.

Spoon the cake batter into the prepared pan and bake for 1¼ hours until golden and well risen.

Serve with a dusting of icing sugar if desired.

CHESTNUT, CHOCOLATE & HAZELNUT CAKE

Torta di castagne, cioccolato e nocciole

This is perfect as an alternative to Christmas cake. It has a celebratory feel with the inclusion of orange, chestnut and brandy. It can also be made dairy free very successfully by using plant-based alternatives.

250 g/2 cups cooked chestnuts

150 ml/²⁄₃ cup full-fat/whole milk

75 g/2³⁄₄ oz. dark/bittersweet chocolate (70% cocoa solids), roughly chopped

50 g/¹⁄₃ cup hazelnuts, toasted and chopped

60 g/¹⁄₄ cup/¹⁄₂ stick unsalted butter, softened

125 g/²⁄₃ cup caster/superfine sugar

3 large/US extra-large eggs, separated

1 tablespoon brandy

grated zest of ¹⁄₂ orange

100 g/3¹⁄₂ oz. sweetened chestnut spread

100 g/¹⁄₂ cup crème fraîche

icing/confectioners' sugar, for dusting (optional)

18-cm/7-inch cake pan, greased and lined

Serves 6–8

Preheat the oven to 180°C/160°C fan/350°F/Gas 4.

Soak the chestnuts in the milk for 10–15 minutes until soft, then drain and discard the milk.

Whizz the chocolate in a food processor until it forms a coarse paste, then set aside. Rinse out the processor, then add the chestnuts and hazelnuts and blend to a rough paste. Set aside.

Put the butter and sugar in the processor and cream together until smooth. Add the egg yolks, one at a time, then add the brandy and orange zest. When everything is well combined, transfer to a large bowl and fold in the chocolate and the chestnut mixture.

Whisk the egg whites to stiff peaks and beat 2 tablespoons into the cake mixture to loosen, then fold in the rest. Tip the mixture into the prepared pan, level the surface and bake for 30 minutes until risen and firm to the touch. Leave to cool for 10 minutes, then carefully turn out onto a wire rack. Remove the baking paper and leave to cool completely.

Swirl the chestnut spread through the crème fraîche and serve with the cake, lightly dusted with icing sugar, if wished.

FRAGRANT COFFEE & CINNAMON LOAF CAKE

Torta al caffè e cannella

This cake is the perfect combination of flavours and really easy to make and to enjoy. Coffee cakes are always winners in my eyes. This is one of my most requested recipes.

175 g/³⁄₄ cup plus 1 teaspoon/
1¹⁄₂ sticks unsalted butter,
softened

160 g/³⁄₄ cup plus 2 teaspoons
soft light brown sugar

3 large/US extra-large eggs

3 tablespoons cold Italian
espresso coffee

2 teaspoons ground cinnamon

175 g/1¹⁄₃ cups Italian 00 flour

2 teaspoons baking powder

FROSTING

150 g/²⁄₃ cup/1¹⁄₄ sticks unsalted
butter, softened

1¹⁄₂ teaspoons ground cinnamon,
plus extra to finish if liked

2 tablespoons cold Italian
espresso coffee

300 g/2 cups icing/
confectioners' sugar

2 teaspoons vanilla extract

20 x 9.5-cm/8 x 3³⁄₄-inch loaf pan,
greased

Serves 12

Preheat the oven to 180°C/160°C fan/350°F/Gas 4.

Whisk the butter and sugar together until light and fluffy using a handheld mixer or stand mixer.

Add the eggs one by one, mixing until well combined. Add the coffee and cinnamon, then sift over the flour and baking powder and gently fold until well combined. The mixture should be damp, with a plopping consistency.

Pour the mixture into the prepared loaf pan and bake for about 20–25 minutes until golden. Leave in the pan to cool for 8 minutes, then turn out onto a wire rack to cool completely.

Make the frosting by combining the butter, cinnamon, coffee, icing sugar and vanilla together in a food processor or stand mixer. Adjust the flavours to your liking.

When the cake is cold, spread the frosting over the top and sides. Add an extra sprinkling of cinnamon to finish if you love the flavour, like me.

CHOCOLATE SIN CAKE
Torta al cioccolato

I first encountered this cake in Sicily. I was so curious I had to try it and it has become a regular feature in my repertoire since. The combination of chocolate and coffee and it's squidginess make this irresistible.

6 large/US extra-large eggs

200 g/1 cup soft brown sugar

250 g/9 oz. dark/bittersweet chocolate

2 teaspoons vanilla extract

1 teaspoon sea salt

1½ tablespoons cold Italian espresso coffee

unsweetened cocoa powder, for dusting

poached fruit and crème fraîche, to serve (optional)

25-cm/10-inch cake pan, greased and floured or lined

Serves 10

Preheat the oven to 180°C/160°C fan/350°F/Gas 4.

Melt the chocolate in a heatproof bowl set over a pan of simmering water (making sure the base of the bowl doesn't touch the water). Add the vanilla and salt to the chocolate, then add the coffee, mix and leave to cool.

Whisk the eggs and sugar together for 8 minutes until thick and creamy using a handheld mixer or stand mixer. Add the chocolate mixture to the egg and sugar in the mixer and mix well on a low-speed.

Pour the batter into the prepared pan and bake for 30 minutes. Leave to cool in the pan. Dust with cocoa and enjoy – it is ridiculously good.

SPICED PEAR & WALNUT CAKE
Ciambellone

4 large/US extra-large eggs, separated

120 g/½ cup plain/natural yoghurt

110 ml/scant ½ cup olive oil

200 g/1 cup caster/superfine sugar

2 teaspoons vanilla extract

finely grated zest of 2 lemons

4 teaspoons ground ginger

2 teaspoons mixed spice

2 teaspoons ground sweet cinnamon

100 g/1 cup toasted and finely chopped walnuts

2 pears, peeled and chopped into 1-cm/½-inch chunks

330 g/2½ cups Italian 00 flour

4 teaspoons baking powder

½ teaspoon sea salt

icing/confectioners' sugar, for dusting

whipped ricotta, to serve

2.4-litre/quart bundt pan, very well greased (see Note on page 38)

Serves 12

Preheat the oven to 180°C/160°C fan/350°F/Gas 4.

Whisk the egg whites in a large bowl until stiff.

In a separate large bowl, beat together the yoghurt, oil, sugar and egg yolks, then add the vanilla, lemon zest, spices, nuts and pears.

Stir in the flour, baking powder and salt and beat until smooth. Gently fold in the egg whites until mixed.

Pour the batter into the prepared bundt pan and bake in the preheated oven for 35 minutes until well risen and golden. Remove from the oven and allow the cake to cool in the pan before inverting onto a wire rack to cool completely. When completely cool, dust the top with icing sugar and serve with whipped ricotta. Excellent enjoyed with a coffee.

Dairy free and wonderfully moist, this is a showstopper of a cake. In Italy, we would serve it as a *merenda* (snack) or enjoy a slice in a *pasticceria* with a coffee. Pecans are a wonderful substitute for the walnuts, if preferred.

RHUBARB, ROSEMARY & PISTACHIO STRUDEL CAKE

Strudel di rabarbaro, rosmarino e pistacchio

Rhubarb is not indigenous to Italy – *strangeri* (English people who have moved to Italy) have made it very popular indeed. It grows better in the north than the south of the country. Rhubarb can be substituted for apples, if preferred.

120 g/½ cup unsalted butter

125 g/½ cup plus 2 tablespoons light brown soft sugar

1 tablespoon finely chopped rosemary

2 large/US extra-large eggs

75 g/¾ cup ground almonds

125 g/1 cup Italian 00 flour

1 teaspoon baking powder

300 g/10½ oz. fresh rhubarb, chopped into 2-cm/1-inch pieces

icing/confectioners' sugar, for dusting

ice cream, to serve (optional)

CRUMBLE TOPPING

50 g/3½ tablespoons unsalted butter

75 g/½ cup Italian 00 flour

75 g/⅓ cup light brown soft sugar

50 g/½ cup finely chopped pistachios

a 23-cm/9-inch springform cake pan, greased and lined

Serves 8–12

Preheat the oven to 180°C/160°C fan/350°F/Gas 4.

In a stand mixer or mixing bowl using an electric whisk, mix the butter with the sugar and the rosemary until light and fluffy.

Add the eggs, one at a time, then add the almonds, flour and baking powder. Mix well and then spoon the batter into the prepared pan.

Make the crumble by mixing the butter, flour and sugar together until it clumps together and resembles large breadcrumbs, then stir in the pistachios. Sprinkle half of the crumble mixture on top, then scatter the rhubarb pieces over the surface and top with the remaining crumble.

Bake in the preheated oven for 50 minutes until golden. Leave to cool in the pan for a few minutes, then turn out onto a wire rack to cool completely. Dust with icing sugar and enjoy with ice cream, if desired.

STRAWBERRY CAKE
Torta di fragole

This is a super light sponge cake that absorbs syrups and alcohol very well indeed.
Using potato flour gives featherlight texture and is available at health food stores.

6 large/US extra-large eggs, separated

150 g/¾ cup golden caster/
   superfine sugar

grated zest of 1 lemon

2 teaspoons vanilla extract

160 g/1¼ cups potato flour, sifted

SYRUP

2 tablespoons raspberry jam

3 tablespoons rum or dry Marsala

TOPPING

400 g/14 oz. strawberries, quartered

grated zest of 1 lemon

lemon verbena leaves

deep, 23-cm/9-inch cake pan,
   greased and lined

Serves 8–10

Preheat the oven to 180°C/160°C fan/350°F/Gas 4.

Whisk the eggs and sugar together for 8 minutes until thick and creamy using a handheld mixer or stand mixer.

Whisk the egg whites to firm, not stiff, peaks. Fold the whites into the egg yolk mixture, then add the lemon zest and vanilla. Sift in the potato flour, then fold into the egg mixture.

Pour the batter into the prepared pan and bake in the preheated oven for about 30 minutes until golden. Leave to cool on a wire rack.

To make the syrup, heat the jam and rum or marsala in a saucepan with 3 tablespoons water until melted. Spoon the syrup over the cake while it is still warm.

Decorate the cake with strawberries, grated lemon zest and lemon verbena when cold.

Note: *Please feel free to use other seasonal fruits if preferred.*

BLOOD ORANGE & ALMOND CAKE
Torta di arance rosse e mandorle

280 g/1¼ cups/2½ sticks unsalted
   butter

225 g/1 cup plus 2 tablespoons
   caster/superfine sugar

6 large/US extra-large eggs, separated

175 g/scant 2 cups ground almonds

175 g/1 cup plus 2 tablespoons coarse
   polenta/cornmeal

zest and juice of 4 blood oranges

blood orange slices and chopped
   almonds, to decorate (optional)

25-cm/10-inch loose bottomed
   round cake pan, greased and lined

Serves 8–12

Preheat the oven to 180°C/160°C fan/350°F/Gas 4. Grease and line the base and sides of the cake pan with baking parchment.

Cream the butter and sugar together in a large bowl until thick and creamy. Add the egg yolks one at a time, beating between each addition. Add the almonds, polenta and orange juice and zest to the mixture and mix together well.

Whisk the egg whites in a clean separate bowl until stiff. Using a metal spoon, fold the whites into the mixture.

Pour the mixture into the prepared pan and bake in the preheated oven for about 50 minutes until golden and firm to the touch. Leave to cool on a wire rack in the pan, and remove from the pan when cool. Decorate with orange slices and toasted flaked almonds before serving, if liked.

There are many variations of this cake – I do hope you like mine. You would think this should only be made in the blood orange season, which is relatively short, starting just after Christmas, and finishing in March in Italy. But normal oranges will give fantastic results, and I have recently been absolutely tantalized by tangerine or clementine juice, which work wonderfully well too. Another gluten-free cake that always hits the spot.

HAZELNUT CAKE
Torta di nocciole

Hazelnuts are probably the most favoured nuts in Italy. They are used in many biscuits/cookies and cakes, and Frangelico – a hazelnut liqueur sold in a friar-shaped bottle – is a great hit with all who try it. This cake is a classic from Piedmont, at the foot of the mountains. I like to think that hazelnuts create a source of energy for the farmers there during the autumn/fall and winter, as they never seem to stop at that time of year: hazelnuts are harvested in august and *vendemmia* (grape harvest) is immediately after, followed by the olive harvest.

300 g/2⅓ cups hazelnuts

200 g/1½ cups Italian 00 flour

2 teaspoons baking powder

3 large/US extra-large eggs

150 g/¾ cup golden caster/
   superfine sugar

100 g/scant ½ cup/1 stick unsalted
   butter, melted and cooled
   to room temperature

3½ tablespoons cold Italian
   espresso coffee

2 tablespoons whole/full-fat milk

2 tablespoons light rum

1 tablespoon olive oil

1 teaspoon vanilla extract

8 amaretti cookies, crushed

icing/confectioners' sugar,
   for dusting

crème fraîche, to serve

23-cm/9-inch cake pan,
   greased and lined

Serves 6

Preheat the oven to 190°C/170°C fan/375°F/Gas 5.

Spread the hazelnuts out on a baking sheet and toast them in the preheated oven for 10 minutes until golden brown. Leave to cool completely. Reserve 2 tablespoons of the toasted hazelnuts for decoration, then finely grind the rest in a food processor.

Sift the flour and baking powder together.

Beat the eggs and sugar in a large bowl for 1 minute using an electric mixer on high speed. Switch the speed to low and blend in the melted butter, coffee, milk, rum, olive oil and vanilla.

When well blended, stir in the ground hazelnuts and amaretti biscuits. Add the flour to the mixture and gently fold in.

Pour the mixture into the prepared cake pan. Bake in the centre of the preheated oven for about 40–45 minutes. Leave to cool for 10 minutes, then turn out onto a cooling rack to cool completely. Dust with icing sugar, top with the reserved hazelnuts and serve with crème fraîche if desired.

ITALIAN BIRTHDAY CAKE
Torta di compleanno

This is perfect for big family gatherings, which happen often in my family. Ideal for anything from an eighteenth birthday, right through to a wedding celebration.

175 g/³⁄₄ cup plus 1 teaspoon/
   1¹⁄₂ sticks unsalted butter
175 g/³⁄₄ cup plus 2 tablespoons
   golden caster/superfine sugar
grated zest of 2 lemons
3 large/US extra-large eggs
175 g/1¹⁄₃ cups Italian 00 flour
2 teaspoons baking powder
3 tablespoons lemon juice

ICING & FILLING
100 g/3¹⁄₂ oz. white chocolate
40 g/3 tablespoons unsalted butter
150 g/1 cup icing/
   confectioners' sugar
4 tablespoons lemon curd
   (or jam or conserve)
50 g/¹⁄₂ cup pistachios,
   finally chopped
50 g/¹⁄₃ cup raspberries

2 x 20-cm/8-inch cake pans,
   greased and lined
birthday candles

Serves 8–12

Preheat the oven to 180°C/160°C fan/350°F/Gas 4.

Cream the butter and sugar with the lemon zest in a stand mixer, or use a handheld mixer, until pale and fluffy. Add the eggs, one at a time, beating well between each addition.

Sift the flour and baking powder onto the egg mixture, adding the lemon juice and mix well to form a dropping consistency. This always makes for a light cake.

Divide the mixture evenly between the two prepared cake pans and bake in the preheated oven for 25–30 minutes until well risen. Leave to cool in the pans for 5 minutes, then turn out onto a wire rack to cool completely.

Melt the chocolate in a heatproof bowl over a pan of simmering water, then leave to cool for 5 minutes. Beat the melted chocolate into the butter, then gradually beat in the icing sugar, adding 1 tablespoon of water if needed to loosen the icing.

Cut each cake in half horizontally and spread the lemon curd on one side and the icing on the other and sandwich together so you have two sponges. Spread lemon curd on top of one sandwiched cake, and icing on the base of the other and sandwich the two cakes together to create a four-layer cake.

Spread the remaining icing all over the top and sides of the cake and press the pistachios onto the sides. Decorate the top with raspberries and candles and celebrate!

Note: *Use pistachio cream (see page 158) as an alternative filling, if preferred.*

APPLE & VANILLA CAKE

Torta di mele

The perfect showstopper for a special celebration.

280 g/scant 1½ cups caster/
    superfine sugar
seeds scraped from 2 vanilla
    pods/beans
200 g/¾ cup/1¾ sticks butter,
    softened, plus 1½ tablespoons
    melted butter for drizzling
1½ teaspoons ground cinnamon
2 large/US extra-large eggs,
    plus 1 egg yolk
375 g/2¾ cups plus 1½ tablespoons
    Italian 00 flour
2 teaspoons baking powder
200 ml/¾–1 cup buttermilk
2 Granny Smith apples, thinly sliced
    into rounds

VANILLA CUSTARD
300 ml/1¼ cups whole/full-fat milk
60 ml/¼ cup dessert wine
1 vanilla pod/bean, split lengthways
110 g/generous ½ cup caster/
    superfine sugar
5 egg yolks
200 g/1½ cups plain/all-purpose flour
200 g/2 cups cornflour/cornstarch

APPLE VANILLA COMPOTE
330 g/1¾ cups caster/superfine sugar
75 ml/⅓ cup brandy
5 small Granny Smith apples,
    each cut into 8 thin wedges.
grated zest and juice of 1 lemon
icing/confectioners' sugar, to dust

20-cm/8-inch cake pan,
    greased with butter
23-cm/9-inch cake pan,
    greased and lined

Serves 10–12

For the vanilla custard, bring the milk, wine and vanilla pod and seeds to a simmer in a saucepan over a medium-high heat. Whisk together the sugar and egg yolks in a bowl, then add both flours and whisk until smooth. Slowly add the hot milk mixture, whisking to combine, then return the mixture to the pan. Bring to the boil, whisking continuously, for 2–3 minutes until thick. Discard the vanilla pod and pour into the prepared 20-cm/8-inch cake pan. Smooth the top and refrigerate for 1–2 hours until firm.

For the apple vanilla compote, stir all the ingredients and 180 ml/¾ cup water in a saucepan over a medium-high heat until the sugar dissolves. Bring to the boil, reduce the heat to medium and simmer for 10–15 minutes until the apples are tender and a syrup forms. Strain, reserving the apples and syrup separately, and refrigerate the apples for about 30 minutes until cool.

Preheat the oven to 180°C/160°C fan/350°F/Gas 4.

Rub 4 teaspoons of the sugar and half the vanilla seeds in a bowl with your fingertips to combine, then set aside.

Beat the butter, remaining sugar, cinnamon and remaining vanilla seeds in an electric mixer for 5 minutes until pale and fluffy. Scrape down the sides of the bowl, then add the eggs and yolk one at a time, beating well after each addition. Add half the flour, then the buttermilk, then the remaining flour, beating between each addition.

Spread half the mixture into the prepared 23-cm/9-inch cake pan.

Unmould the vanilla custard and place in the centre of the larger pan. Spoon over the apple compote, followed by the remaining cake batter over the top. Smooth the top, then arrange the sliced apples in a circle, overlapping the edges. Drizzle with the melted butter, scatter with vanilla sugar, then bake for 1½–1¾ hours until golden and cooked though (cover with foil partway through cooking if the cake starts to brown too quickly and remove the foil for the last 10 minutes of cooking).

Leave to stand for 30 minutes in the pan, then run a small knife around the side and turn out onto a rack to cool for 30 minutes. Serve warm, drizzled with the reserved syrup.

RASPBERRY, ORANGE, LEMON & YOGURT CAKE

Torta alla yogurt, limone, arancia e lampone

Deliciously light and moist, you can even use out-of-date yogurt.

4 large/US extra-large eggs, separated

120 g/½ cup natural/plain yogurt

110 ml/½ cup olive oil

200 g/1 cup caster/superfine sugar

finely grated zest of 1 orange

finely grated zest of 1 lemon

2 teaspoons vanilla extract

330 g/2½ cups Italian 00 flour

½ teaspoon salt

2 teaspoons baking powder

150 g/1 cup raspberries, plus extra
   to serve

icing/confectioners' sugar, for dusting

23-cm/9-inch cake pan, bundt pan
   or ring mould, greased and lined

Serves 8–12

Preheat oven to 180°C/160°C fan/350°F/Gas 4.

Beat the egg whites in a medium bowl until stiff.

In a separate large bowl, beat the yogurt, oil, sugar and egg yolks with the orange and lemon zest. Stir in the vanilla, flour, salt, baking powder and raspberries, then fold in the egg whites, incorporating evenly.

Pour the batter into the prepared pan or mould. Bake for 35–40 minutes until golden and the cake has pulled away from the sides of the pan.

Leave to cool before releasing the cake from the pan. Dust with icing sugar, top with extra fresh raspberries and enjoy.

Note: *If you are using a bundt pan, it is best to use a cake release spray or liquid to coat the inside of the pan before use (I use a brilliant one called PME Release-a-Cake from Lakeland.com).*

ROSEMARY & ORANGE HONEY CAKE

Torta al miele di arancia e rosmarino

3 large/US extra-large eggs

pinch of sea salt

5 tablespoons orange blossom honey
   (or your favourite type)

1 tablespoon finely chopped rosemary

75 ml/⅓ cup olive oil

grated zest and juice of 2 oranges

300 g/2¼ cups Italian 00 flour

1 tablespoon baking powder

icing/confectioners' sugar, for dusting

orange slices and rosemary sprigs,
   to decorate (optional)

26-cm/10¼-inch loose-bottomed
   cake pan, greased and lined

Serves 6–8

Preheat the oven to 190C/170°C fan/375°F/Gas 5.

Mix the eggs and salt together with a whisk until thickened. Add the honey, rosemary, oil and orange zest and juice and mix well. Add the flour and baking powder and stir well until blended.

Spoon the mixture into the prepared pan and bake for 35 minutes until a skewer comes out clean when inserted in the centre.

Leave to cool in the pan for 5 minutes, then turn out onto a wire rack to cool completely. Dust with icing sugar to finish and decorate with orange slices and rosemary sprigs, if liked.

I'm enraptured with honey.
I have always admired the
bees that make honey, the
history, the taste and of
course the bee keepers.
This cake is a mixture of
Nonna Ferrigno and my time
spent in Tuscany. Please
spend your money wisely
and buy good, real honey –
using spectacular honey
will make a huge difference
to your cake.

PEACH & PISTACHIO SLICE
Torta rovesciata con pesche e pistacchi

A strong recipe for a novice baker as the method is simple and easy to master. Milk provides a tender crumb for all cakes, and this is no exception. Adding pistachios makes this a bright, colourful, cheerful cake to enjoy in the Italian apricot season.

185 g/1⅓ cups Italian 00 flour

170 g/¾ cup plus 1½ tablespoons caster/superfine sugar, plus 2 tablespoons extra for sprinkling

1 teaspoon baking powder

pinch of salt

50 g/scant ½ cup pistachios, chopped, plus extra to decorate

3 large/US extra-large eggs

60 ml/¼ cup milk

2 teaspoons vanilla extract

grated zest of 1 lemon

180 g/¾ cup plus 2 teaspoons/ 1½ sticks butter, softened

14 apricots, stoned/pitted and halved

20 x 30-cm/8 x 12-inch baking pan, greased

Makes 14 slices

Preheat the oven to 160°C/140°C fan/325°F/Gas 3.

Sift the flour into a large bowl, add the sugar, baking powder, salt and pistachios and make a well in the centre.

Put the eggs, milk, vanilla and lemon zest in another bowl and mix to combine. Pour the egg mixture into the well in the dry ingredients, add the butter and beat for 2 minutes until smooth.

Spread the mixture evenly into the baking pan. Push the apricot halves, cut side up, into the cake mixture in four even rows of seven. Bake in the oven for 20 minutes.

Sprinkle over the extra sugar and cook for another 20 minutes or until a skewer inserted into the centre comes out clean. Decorate with pistachios and cut the cake into fingers with two apricot halves per slice to serve.

CAPPUCCINO LOAF CAKE
Torta al cappuccino

This is my go-to cake when I'm really busy and just need a cake
to keep me going or to offer to friends who might happen to pop in.

5 tablespoons single/
   light cream
2–3 tablespoons cold
   Italian espresso coffee
   (or to taste)
175 g/³/₄ cup/1¹/₂ sticks
   unsalted butter, softened,
100 g/¹/₂ cup golden caster/
   superfine sugar
75 g/¹/₃ cup light brown
   muscovado sugar
3 large/US extra-large eggs
1 teaspoon vanilla extract

175 g/1¹/₃ cups Italian
   00 flour
¹/₂ teaspoon salt
1¹/₂ teaspoon baking powder

CAPPUCCINO FROSTING
150 g/5¹/₂ oz./²/₃ cup
   mascarpone
5 tablespoons icing/
   confectioners' sugar
cocoa powder, for dusting

900-g/2-lb. loaf pan,
   greased and lined

Serves 10

Preheat the oven to 170°C/150°C fan/325°F/Gas 3.

Mix the cream and coffee together in a small bowl.

In a separate bowl, mix 1 teaspoon of the coffee
cream with the mascarpone for the frosting and
chill until needed.

In a large bowl, using electric beaters, cream the
butter with the two sugars for 3–4 minutes until pale
and fluffy. Beat in the eggs one at a time, followed
by the vanilla and the remaining coffee cream.

Fold in the flour, salt and baking powder until you
have a smooth batter. Scrape into the prepared pan
and bake for 45–50 minutes until a skewer inserted
into the centre comes out clean. Leave in the pan
to cool for a few minutes, then turn out onto a wire
rack to cool to room temperature.

Meanwhile, make the frosting. Sift the icing sugar
over the chilled coffee mascarpone and whisk with
electric beaters for 1–2 minutes until silky. Chill
again until needed.

Spread the frosting over the cooled cake and dust
lightly with cocoa powder just before serving.

Note: *Using baking powder rather than self-raising
flour means you will get a much more potent mix
in a bake, as self-raising flour can be quite old and
lose it's punch.*

GENOESE SPONGE CAKE
Torta pasta genovese

This light sponge is ideal to use as the base for Italian gateaux. It can simply be filled with cream or used for making zuccotto (see page 126) and cassata (see page 122).

55 g/3½ tablespoons unsalted butter

4 large/US extra-large eggs

115 g/½ cup plus 1 tablespoon caster/superfine sugar

pinch of salt

115 g/¾ cup plus 2 tablespoons plain/all-purpose or Italian 00 flour

whipped cream and berry compote, to serve (optional)

deep, 23-cm/9-inch cake pan, greased and lined

Serves 8–10

Preheat the oven to 180°C/160°C fan/350°F/Gas 4.

Melt the butter, then set aside to cool.

Put the eggs, sugar and salt in a heatproof bowl set over a saucepan of gently simmering water. Whisk until the mixture is thick, pale and tripled in volume. Remove the bowl from the heat and continue to whisk until the mixture is cool.

Sift some of the flour over the top of the mixture. Slowly trickle in some of the cooled, melted butter around the edge of the bowl, then, using a metal spoon, gently fold in both ingredients. Repeat until all the flour and butter are used up. It is essential you maintain a mousse-like consistency.

Pour the mixture into the prepared pan and bake for 25–30 minutes until golden brown, firm to the touch and shrunk slightly from the sides of the pan. Leave to cool in the pan for 1–2 minutes, then turn out onto a wire rack to cool completely. Serve with cream and berry compote if wished.

ITALIAN PLUM CAKE

Torta di prugne

This cake is enjoyed all over Italy. I think the name has been lost in translation though, as there are no plums included! Perfect served as a *merenda* (snack) or for breakfast.

200 g/¾ cup/1¾ sticks unsalted butter

200 g/1 cup caster/superfine sugar

4 large/US extra-large eggs, separated

2 teaspoons vanilla extract

250 g/1¾ cups plus 2 tablespoons Italian 00 flour

1 teaspoon baking powder

pinch of salt

icing/confectioners' sugar, for dusting

900-g/2-lb. loaf pan, greased and lined

Serves 8–10

Preheat the oven to 170°C/150°C fan/325°F/Gas 3.

Cream the butter and sugar together in a mixing bowl until light and fluffy. This is always an important job. Add the egg yolks, one at a time, and mix well between each addition. Stir through the vanilla.

Mix the flour, baking powder and salt together, then mix into the creamed mixture. Beat the egg whites in a clean bowl until stiff peaks form. Fold the egg whites into the mixture. Spoon the batter into the prepared loaf pan and bake in the preheated oven for 40 minutes until golden and well risen. Cool on a wire rack, then dust with icing sugar before serving.

Note: *This cake benefits from a hard mix and being made in a stand mixer.*

TARTS & SWEET BREADS

Crostate e pani dolci

The sweet smell of baking pastry

Every village, town and city in Italy boasts entrancing and enticing food shops, with products arranged artistically and colourfully in the front window. Think of the bars offering a choice of *cicchetti* in Venice, the *gelaterie* proudly displaying their jewel-like ice-creams, and pastry-shops and bakeries – *pasticcerie* and *panetterie* respectively – have displays that are no less tantalizing. The Italians love food, and they love their foods, sweet or savoury, to be presented beautifully.

Most Italians buy tarts from *pasticcerie* on a regular basis. They might choose a slice to go with their morning espresso, or to have as an afternoon snack,

or *merenda*. Or they might choose a whole tart, which can be served as a special-occasion dessert. The pastry used professionally, and at home, is a sweet shortcrust known as *pasta frolla*, which consists basically of Italian 00 flour, butter and sugar. However, each region, shop or indeed household, might have its own take on the basic recipe, and there are numerous ingredients that can be added, such as eggs, ground nuts, finely grated citrus peel, cocoa powder, pure vanilla extract, sometimes even alcohol! The recipe I give you on page 54 is one my mother used to make, and it is truly delicious. There are a couple of other pastries here as well, as often the pastry type is dependent on the filling you are going to marry with it. It's basically common sense: the more liquid the filling, the denser the pastry should be, and vice versa.

These are some basic rules for making and working with pastry. Never over-work pastry as this will make it heavy: be light fingered! And always chill pastry.

Chill it for about 30 minutes, wrapped in cling film/ plastic wrap, after you make it, then again after rolling and shaping. If the pastry is not cold enough, it will shrink in the oven heat; you could even put the pastry-lined pan briefly in the freezer!

Many pastry tart bases are cooked raw, with the filling in; other tart cases/shells are pre- or blind-baked, which makes them crisper. Use baking paper or foil to line the pastry-lined pan, pour in commercial baking beans (or use some rice or pulses that you can keep specially for blind-baking), and bake for the time suggested.

The fillings for Italian tarts, big and small, vary enormously. Often the base will be a type of custard, which I talk about on page 88, and cream and chocolate are involved too. The usual accompaniments to these bases are fruits, many of which grow so prolifically in Italy – peaches, pears, strawberries, plums, figs, apricots – but there are many tarts made with nuts and jams as well. You will find a good selection here to choose from.

Bread is one of the major strands of Italian cooking. Sweet breads are more of a festive or special-occasion food, and some of the most famous Italian sweet breads are associated with religious festivals: the Milanese panettone with Christmas, for instance, and *pandolce* with Easter. Some are connected to season: the flatbread with grapes on page 81, is traditionally eaten after the *vendemmia*, when the grapes have been picked. Some breads here are not actually sweet because they contain a lot of sugar, but because they contain so much dried fruit (condensed sweetness!). Many sweet breads are eaten in a savoury context – with cheese or dips, for instance – and I love a slice of my lemon bread at breakfast.

Although I have a separate chapter about sweet things to make as gifts, never forget that a home-baked tart or sweet bread would make a wonderful present. Nothing is quite so special as something a friend has spent time and effort on.

STICKY PLUM, HAZELNUT & ALMOND TART

Torta di prugne, mandorle e nocciole

I use this fantastic pastry in many of my tarts as it is so easy to make and foolproof. It is my mummy's pastry recipe, passed down from her mother, so holds a very special place in my heart. Please feel free to use other seasonal fruits, and even nuts, if liked, to make this recipe your own.

PASTA FROLLA

250 g/1¾ cups plus 2 tablespoons
   Italian 00 flour or white spelt
   flour, plus extra for dusting

75 g/½ cup icing/
   confectioners' sugar

125 g/½ cup plus 1 tablespoon
   chilled unsalted butter

1 large/US extra-large egg

pinch of salt

few drops of vanilla extract

grated zest of 1 lemon

FILLING

150 g/⅔ cup/1¼ sticks
   unsalted butter, softened

100 g/½ cup golden caster/
   superfine sugar

grated zest of 1 lemon

3 large/US extra-large eggs

50 g/½ cup ground almonds

75 g/½ cup plus 1 tablespoon
   Italian 00 flour

¾ teaspoon baking powder

1 teaspoon vanilla extract

400 g/14 oz. ripe plums, quartered
   or halved (or use chopped
   apples or pears)

2 tablespoons flaked almonds

2 tablespoons apricot jam

deep, 23-cm/9-inch loose-
   bottomed tart pan

Serves 12

First, make the pastry. Place all of the ingredients in a food processor and pulse to mix. Turn out onto a lightly floured surface and knead into a smooth dough. Flatten slightly, wrap in cling film/plastic wrap and set aside for 30 minutes in the fridge.

Preheat the oven to 180°C/160°C fan/350°F/Gas 4.

Roll out the pastry thinly on a floured board and use it to line the pan (there will be some leftover pastry, see note below). Chill in the fridge for 10 minutes.

In a medium bowl, mix together all the filling ingredients, except for the plums, almonds and jam. Spoon the filling into the tart case. Press the plums evenly into the mixture and scatter with the almonds. Bake in the preheated oven for 45 minutes until risen and golden brown.

Melt the apricot jam with 1 tablespoon water in a small saucepan, brush over the top of the tart and leave to cool on a wire rack. Can be served hot, cold or warm.

Note: *You will have enough pastry leftover to make a crostata (small one crust pie) or maybe some jam tarts.*

UMBRIAN STRUDEL
La Rocciata di Assisi

Rocciata is an almost literal translation of *rugelach*, which are 'small Jewish pastries' encasing a variety of fruits and nuts. In this delicious version however, the slices are larger and the pastry is made from a thicker, more elastic dough than usual.

PASTRY
300 g/2¼ cups Italian 00 flour
pinch of sea salt
1 large/US extra-large egg,
   lightly beaten
1 tablespoon olive oil
3 tablespoons warm water

FILLING
2 medium eating apples, peeled,
   cored and thinly sliced
8 dried prunes, stoned/pitted
   and chopped
2 dried figs, stems removed
   and chopped
55 g/½ cup pine nuts, chopped
8 walnuts, shelled and chopped
8 hazelnuts, shelled and chopped
1 teaspoon finely grated lemon zest
1 teaspoon ground cinnamon
85 g/scant ½ cup caster/
   superfine sugar
5 tablespoons Marsala wine

TO SERVE
icing/confectioners' sugar,
   for dusting
dried fruits and nuts, to decorate

large baking sheet, greased
   and lined

Serves 8–10

First, make the pastry. Heap the flour and salt on a work surface and make a well in the centre. Add the egg, oil and 1 tablespoon of the water and mix with a fork, incorporating the flour a little at a time and adding more water as needed to form a soft, smooth dough. Knead the pastry for 10 minutes, then cover with a damp tea/dish towel, and leave to rest for 1 hour.

Preheat the oven to 180°C/160°C fan/350°F/Gas 4.

Put all the filling ingredients into a bowl and mix until they are well blended.

Roll the pastry into a 40 x 50-cm/16 x 20-inch rectangle, about 3 mm/⅛ inch thick. Distribute the fruit-and-nut mixture evenly over the surface, leaving a 4-cm/1½-inch border on all sides. Roll up from the short side and press the edges together to seal them. Arrange the roll on the buttered baking sheet, seam-side down.

Bake in the preheated oven for 30 minutes. Remove from the oven and leave to cool for 15 minutes. Dust with icing sugar and decorate with dried fruits and nuts, then cut into 2.5-cm/1-inch thick slices to serve.

STRAWBERRY TARTLETS
Crostatine di fragole

These tartlets are typical of Italy and found in so many *pasticceria*.
Use this recipe to experiment with different fruits when in season;
my father loved it with whole black cherries and cherry conserve.
Hazelnuts would also be a lovely addition.

PASTRY

300 g/2¼ cups plain/all-purpose
   or Italian 00 flour, plus extra
   for dusting
pinch of salt
150 g/²⁄₃ cup/1¼ sticks unsalted
   butter, softened
100 g/½ cup caster/superfine sugar
1 large/US extra-large egg and
   3 egg yolks
freshly grated zest of 1 lemon

FILLING

275 g/10 oz. strawberry high-fruit-
   content conserve
450 g/1 lb. strawberries, halved
   or quartered if large, pus extra
   to decorate
edible flowers, to decorate
icing/confectioners' sugar,
   for dusting

12-cm/5-inch cookie cutter
8 x 10-cm/4-inch tartlet pans

Makes 8

For the pastry, put the flour and salt into a bowl with the butter, sugar, egg and egg yolks and lemon zest. Using your fingertips, knead the ingredients together to form a soft dough. Wrap in non-stick baking paper and chill in the fridge for 30 minutes.

Preheat the oven to 190°C/170°C fan/375°F/Gas 5.

On a lightly floured surface, roll out three-quarters of the pastry, cut out rounds with the cookie cutter and use them to line the tartlet pans. Spread each pastry case with the strawberry conserve and top strawberries.

Roll out the remaining pastry, cut into strips and use to form a lattice on top of each tartlet.

Bake in the oven for 18–20 minutes until golden, then leave to cool in the pans.

Before serving, decorate with strawberries and flowers and dust with icing sugar.

PINE NUT TART
Torta della Nonna

This tart is enjoyed throughout Italy and many *pasticceria* will sell a slice with a coffee for breakfast or to take home. This particular recipe is the very best I know, although there are many regional variations. Please do use fresh pine nuts and store in the fridge to prevent them from becoming rancid. There is a huge difference in flavour between Asian and Mediterranean pine nuts – try to find Mediterranean ones if you can.

PASTRY
150 g/²/₃ cup/1¼ sticks unsalted
    butter, softened
150 g/¾ cup caster/superfine sugar
4 large/US extra-large egg yolks
350 g/2²/₃ cups plain/all-purpose
    or Italian 00 flour, plus extra
    for dusting
grated zest of 1 lemon
pinch of salt

FILLING
350 g/1½ cups ricotta
few drops of vanilla extract
50 ml/scant ¼ cup double/
    heavy cream
3 large/US extra-large egg yolks
100 g/½ cup caster/superfine sugar
100 g/¾ cup pine nuts
icing/confectioners' sugar,
    for dusting

20-cm/8-inch
    loose-bottomed flan pan

Serves 8–12

For the pastry, put the softened butter, sugar and egg yolks in a food processor and mix together. Add the flour, lemon zest and salt and mix again until it comes together into a dough. Wrap in non-stick baking paper and chill in the fridge for 1 hour.

Preheat the oven to 170°C/150°C fan/325°F/Gas 3.

To make the filling, using a wooden spoon, beat the ricotta cheese in a bowl. Add the vanilla extract, cream, egg yolks, sugar and three-quarters of the pine nuts and mix together.

On a lightly floured surface, roll out the pastry and use two-thirds to line the pan. Chill in the fridge for 30 minutes.

Prick the base with a fork, line with a piece of baking paper and top with baking beans. Bake in the oven for about 20 minutes until golden.

Remove the lining and baking beans. Pour the filling into the pastry case.

Roll out the remaining pastry and cut into 1-cm/½-inch strips, the same length as the diameter of the tart. Use the strips to make a lattice decoration by layering half the strips at intervals across the surface and the other half across the first layer. Scatter the remaining pine nuts over the top.

Bake in the oven for 35 minutes until the pastry is crisp and golden and the filling is firm to the touch

Leave to cool slightly, then serve warm, dusted with icing sugar.

INDIVIDUAL FRESH FRUIT TARTLETS

Crostatine di frutta fresca

There is something very appealing about little tartlets filled with pastry cream and topped with fresh fruit. Choose small fruits and berries when they come into season.

fresh seasonal fruits, such as
  strawberries, raspberries, figs,
  grapes, peaches, apricots
60 g/¼ cup apricot conserve
1 tablespoon white rum

PASTRY
350 g/2⅔ cups plain/all-purpose
  or Italian 00 flour, plus extra
  for dusting
175 g/¾ cup/1½ sticks unsalted
  butter, softened
175 g/scant 1 cup caster/
  superfine sugar
grated zest of 1 lemon
120 ml/½ cup white rum
pinch of salt

PASTRY CREAM
3 large/US extra-large eggs
75 g/⅓ cup caster/superfine sugar
40 g/scant ½ cup cornflour/
  cornstarch
450 ml/scant 2 cups milk
2 teaspoons vanilla extract

12-cm/5-inch cookie cutter
12 x 10-cm/4-inch tartlet pans

Makes 12

To make the pastry, put the flour in a bowl and rub in the butter until the mixture resembles breadcrumbs. Make a well in the centre and add the sugar, lemon zest, rum and salt. Using a fork, mix together to form a ball. Wrap in non-stick baking paper and chill in the fridge for 1 hour.

To make the pastry cream, beat together the eggs and sugar until pale and thick. Sift in the cornflour and beat until smooth. Heat the milk in a saucepan until almost boiling, then pour onto the egg mixture, stirring all the time. Return the mixture to the pan and cook over a low heat, stirring, until the mixture boils and thickens. Add the vanilla extract. Cover the surface with a piece of greaseproof paper and leave the mixture to cool completely.

On a lightly floured surface, roll out the pastry, cut out rounds with the cookie cutter and use them to line the tartlet pans. Line the pastry cases with baking paper and weigh down with baking beans. Chill in the fridge for at least 15 minutes.

Preheat the oven to 180°C/160°C fan/350°F/Gas 4.

Bake the tartlets in the oven for 10 minutes, then remove the baking beans and continue baking for a further 5 minutes until crisp. Transfer to a wire rack and leave to cool.

Fill the tartlets with the pastry cream and top with whole fruit, or slices of fresh fruit. Sieve/strain the apricot conserve into a saucepan and add the rum. Heat gently, then brush the glaze over the top of the fruit. Serve within 2 hours.

CHOCOLATE & PEAR TART
Crostata di pere e cioccolato

This is inspired by the pear harvest in Italy. Although perhaps
unusual in a tart, I just love this combination.

3 tablespoons marmalade

2 ripe pears, cored and cut
into wedges

cocoa powder, for dusting

PASTRY

50 g/3½ tablespoons
unsalted butter

100 g/¾ cup plain/
all-purpose or Italian 00
flour, plus extra for dusting

25 g/¼ cup cocoa powder

50 g/¼ cup caster/
superfine sugar

1 large/US extra-large egg,
beaten

FILLING

100 g/3½ oz. dark/
bittersweet chocolate
(70% cocoa solids)

50 g/3½ tablespoons
unsalted butter

2 large/US extra-large eggs,
separated

100 g/½ cup caster/
superfine sugar

20-cm/8-inch flan pan

Serves 8–12

To make the pastry, rub the butter into the flour until
the mixture resembles breadcrumbs. Sift in the cocoa
powder, add the sugar and enough of the beaten egg
to bind the mixture together. Knead lightly, wrap in
non-stick baking paper and leave to chill in the fridge
for 20 minutes.

Preheat the oven to 180°C/160°C fan/350°F/Gas 4.

On a lightly floured surface, roll out the pastry and use
to line the flan pan. Cover the base with the marmalade.

To make the filling, melt the chocolate and butter in
a heatproof bowl set over a pan of simmering water
over a low heat. Set aside to cool.

Beat together the egg yolks and sugar until pale and
fluffy. Fold in the melted chocolate and butter.

Whisk the egg whites until stiff, then fold them into
the chocolate mixture.

Pour the mixture into the tart case and arrange the
pear wedges on top. Bake in the oven for 40 minutes
until firm to the touch. Serve hot or cold dusted with
cocoa powder to finish.

FIG & GRAPE CROSTATA WITH HAZELNUT CREMA

Crostata di fichi e uva con crema di nocciola

I have an enduring passion for figs and I don't make any apologies for it either, as I just love them. More and more people that I teach seem to have them growing in their gardens and we are now able to buy them for lengthy periods in the supermarkets, so they are readily available for most of the year.

1 quantity of Pasta Frolla dough (see page 54)

3 fresh figs, quartered

20 muscat grapes (preferably seedless)

HAZELNUT CREMA

50 g/3½ tablespoons unsalted butter, softened

50 g/¼ cup caster/superfine sugar

50 g/½ cup toasted ground hazelnuts

50 g/6 tablespoons Italian 00 flour, plus extra for dusting

1 large/US extra-large egg

large baking sheet, lined with baking paper

Serves 8–10

Once you have made your pastry dough, leave it to rest in the fridge for at least 30 minutes.

Preheat the oven to 180°C/160°C fan/350°F/Gas 4.

Now make the crema. Cream together the butter and sugar in a medium bowl until light and fluffy. Add the hazelnuts, flour and egg and mix to a soft cream.

Divide the dough in half (see the Note below for what to do with the other half). Roll one portion of the pastry out on a lightly floured board to a circle that is roughly 26 cm/10¼ inch in diameter.

Place the pastry round on the prepared baking sheet and spread the crema over the top, leaving a 3-cm/1¼-inch rim around the edge. Arrange the cut figs and grapes over the crema in an attractive pattern, then fold the pastry rim over the filling slightly to just cover the filling, as it will sink as it bakes.

Bake in the preheated oven for 25 minutes until golden and juicy. Leave to cool slightly on a wire rack. Enjoy hot or cold.

Notes: *Freeze the remaining dough for another occasion and use within a month. It will be damp when it defrosts, so give it another dusting of flour before using.*

You might like to glaze the crostata with warmed apricot conserve or simply dust with icing/confectioners' sugar before serving.

VERY BERRY TART
Crostata ai frutti di bosco

This tart ensures that we truly enjoy the berry season!

1 quantity of Pasta Frolla dough (see page 54)

45 g/3 tablespoons unsalted butter

90 g/½ cup minus 2 teaspoons caster/superfine sugar

50 g/½ cup ground almonds

40 g/¼ cup Italian 00 flour, plus extra for dusting

1 large/US extra-large egg

1 teaspoon baking powder

handful of raspberries

handful of strawberries, halved

handful of blackberries

icing/confectioners' sugar, for dusting

crème fraîche, to serve

23-cm/9-inch loose-bottomed fluted tart pan

Serves 8–10

Preheat the oven to 160°C/140°C fan/325°F/Gas 3.

Roll out the pastry thinly on a floured surface and use it to line the tart pan, trimming any excess dough. Arrange the berries over the base of the tart.

Mix together the butter, sugar, ground almonds, flour, egg and baking powder in a bowl. Spoon the sponge mixture on top of the berries in the tart pan so they are completely covered.

Bake the tart in the preheated oven for 35 minutes until golden brown, then leave to cool in the pan.

Dust with icing sugar to finish and serve with crème fraîche if liked.

Note: *I sometimes like to serve this tart decorated with edible geranium flowers for an extra flourish.*

BLACKBERRY & CHOCOLATE TART
Crostata di more e cioccolato

I'm really delighted with this flavour combination. Often blackberries can
be quite tart, but when combined with chocolate, they work beautifully.

1 quantity Pasta Frolla
    dough (see page 54)
180 g/6½ oz. dark/
    bittersweet chocolate
    (80% cocoa solids), plus
    extra, grated, to serve
60 g/¼ cup/½ stick
    unsalted butter
3 large/US extra-large eggs,
    separated

50 g/¼ cup caster/
    superfine sugar
60 ml/¼ cup double/
    heavy cream
200 g/7 oz. blackberries,
    plus extra to serve

35 x 11-cm/14 x 4½-inch
loose-bottom tart pan

Serves 8–10

Preheat the oven to 190°C/170°C fan/375°F/Gas 5.

Roll out the pastry thinly on a floured board and use
it to line the pan. Prick the base with a fork, line with
a piece of non-stick baking paper and top with baking
beans. Bake in the preheated oven for 10 minutes
until golden. Remove the lining and baking beans.

Lower the oven temperature to 160°C/140°C fan/
325°F/Gas 3.

Place the chocolate and butter in a heatproof bowl
over a pan of simmering water to melt, stir, then
leave to cool.

Whisk the egg whites with the sugar in a large bowl
until soft peaks form.

Stir the egg yolks into the cooled chocolate mixture,
followed by the egg white and sugar mixture. Stir well
to combine.

Place the blackberries on the base of the pre-cooked
tart case and top with the chocolate filling, smoothing
the surface.

Bake in the oven for 20 minutes. It should still have
a slight wobble, and will set further as it cools. Don't
panic if it cracks or splits during baking, this is normal
and it will relax as it cools.

Top with more blackberries and some grated
chocolate and enjoy.

FIG, AMARETTI & RICOTTA TART

Crostata di fichi, amaretti e ricotta

When the figs are ripe and succulent, this tart demands to be made.
Full of classic Venetian tastes and textures, a small slice with
an espresso is just enough to lift your day.

130 g/½ cup unsalted butter

250 g/9 oz. amaretti biscuits/
   cookies

175 g/6 oz. full-fat soft cheese

500 g/1 lb. 2 oz. ricotta

100 g/½ cup caster/superfine sugar

1 tablespoon vanilla extract

grated zest of 1 lemon

2 tablespoons amaretto liqueur

12 ripe figs, trimmed and sliced
   or quartered

1 teaspoon crushed fennel seeds
   (optional)

deep 23-cm/9-inch loose-
   bottomed tart pan,
   lightly greased

Serves 8–10

Preheat the oven to 170°C/150°C fan/325°F/Gas 3.

Melt the butter in a saucepan. Blitz the amaretti in a food
processor, then add to the pan with the butter and mix well. Tip
the mixture into the base of the pan, then press down with the
back of the spoon to evenly distribute the crumbs and cover the
base and sides of the pan. Bake the tart base in the preheated
oven for about 10 minutes. Leave to cool.

Mix the soft cheese, ricotta, sugar, vanilla extract, lemon zest and
amaretto liqueur together. Spoon the ricotta mixture evenly over
the tart base. Chill in the fridge for at least 3 hours, then top with
the sliced figs in a circular pattern. Scatter over the fennel seeds
to finish, if using.

Note: *You may like to top the tart with a fig leaf syrup as I have
done here. To make the syrup, combine 1 litre/quart water,
3 fig leaves and 150 g/¾ cup caster/superfine sugar, then boil
together until thick and syrupy. Drizzle over the tart to finish.*

MINI CREAM-FILLED BUNS
Maritozzi

A very delicious and popular cream bun from Roma. Despite my appetite, I think slightly smaller *maritozzi* are more appealing. They are perfect for breakfast, brunch, afternoon tea, *merenda* (snack), family gatherings and sharing with friends. The original recipe has just whipped cream as its filling, but feel free to make them as imaginative as you are!

4 g/¹⁄₈ oz. fast action dried yeast (or 8 g/¹⁄₄ oz. fresh yeast)
125 ml/¹⁄₂ cup whole/full-fat milk, warmed to about 37°C/99°F
250 g/1³⁄₄ cups strong bread flour or Italian 00 flour, plus extra for dusting
50 g/¹⁄₄ cup caster/superfine sugar
1 large/US extra-large egg yolk
25 ml/2 tablespoons neutral oil
1 teaspoon vanilla extract
coarsely grated zest of 1 orange

SUGAR GLAZE
25 g/1¹⁄₂ tablespoons golden caster/superfine sugar
¹⁄₂ teaspoon sea salt

FILLING
225 ml/scant 1 cup whipping cream
2 teaspoons icing/confectioners' sugar
¹⁄₂ teaspoon vanilla extract

2 large baking sheets, lined with baking paper
piping/pastry bag
palette knife

Makes 12 buns

Make a sponge starter by mixing the yeast with the warmed milk first until the yeast has dissolved, then mix in half the flour and sugar. Mix well by hand with a whisk, cover and leave for 1 hour until risen, spongy and bubbly.

Combine all the remaining ingredients in a bowl with the sponge starter and add the remaining flour, little by little, mixing to a dough that is not sticky.

Tip the dough out of the bowl onto a lightly floured surface and knead for at least 10 minutes until a smooth dough is formed. This is always my favourite part of bread making – use the time to make mental shopping lists, knead to some music or just relax into this meditative process.

Return the dough to a clean bowl, cover well and leave until doubled in size. Depending on the temperature, this will take about 1 hour at a room temperature above 20°C/68°F.

Knock back the dough to release the gas trapped inside. Shape the dough into a round and divide into 10 even pieces (or weigh into 30-g/1-oz. portions). Shape each piece of dough into an oval by firstly rolling into a ball and very lightly pinching the dough underneath to achieve a smooth shape. Place the dough pieces onto the prepared baking sheets, not too close as they will expand. Cover and leave to rise for 40 minutes.

Preheat the oven 200°C/180°C fan/400°F/Gas 6.

Bake the buns in the preheated oven for 10 minutes until golden brown.

To make the glaze, place the sugar and salt in a saucepan with 2 tablespoons water and heat gently until the sugar has dissolved and the glaze is thickened. Brush the glaze over the buns when they come out of the oven to give them a gorgeous high sheen, then leave the buns to cool on a wire rack.

Whip the cream with the icing sugar and vanilla until thickened. Slice the buns with a bread knife down the middle of each bun. Fill a piping bag with the cream and pipe the cream into each bun to fill. Use a small palette knife to scrape the cream smooth to give the maritozzi its recognizable finish.

Note: *For other fillings, use pistachio cream (see page 158) mixed with cream, a chocolate cream or Nutella, or the spiced fig jam (see page 104) is especially delicious. Press any other decorations that you like into the surface – freeze-dried raspberries, chocolate, chopped nuts or fruits, for example.*

LEMON BREAD
Torta di limone

This bread is totally delicious toasted as a breakfast bread with lashings of butter.

400 g/2¾ cups strong white flour, plus extra for dusting

100 g/¾ cup rye flour

1 tablespoon fine sea salt

70 g/⅓ cup/⅔ stick unsalted butter, softened and diced

70 g/⅓ cup caster/superfine sugar

25 g/1 oz. fresh yeast, crumbled

300 ml/1¼ cups water at body temperature

2 tablespoons olive oil

finely grated zest of 5 lemons

115 g/4 oz. candied lemon peel, finely chopped (preferably homemade, see page 170)

icing/confectioners' sugar, for dusting (optional)

large baking sheet, greased

Makes 2 loaves

Place the flours, salt, butter and sugar into a large bowl. Rub the butter into the dry ingredients until the mixture resembles breadcrumbs, then make a well in the centre.

Cream the yeast with 1 tablespoon of the water and add it to the flour with the olive oil and remaining water. Mix until the dough comes away from the sides of the bowl.

Tip the dough out onto a lightly floured surface and knead for 5 minutes until smooth. Place the dough in a lightly oiled bowl, cover with a damp tea/dish towel and leave to rise for 1 hour, or until it has doubled in size.

Knock the dough back, then knead it for 2–3 minutes on a lightly floured surface before kneading in the lemon zest and candied peel.

Shape the dough into two round loaves and place them on the prepared baking sheet. Make three cuts across each loaf, cover with a damp tea/dish towel and leave to prove for 1 hour, or until they have doubled in size.

Preheat the oven to 200°C/180°C fan/400°F/Gas 6.

Bake the loaves in the oven for 25–30 minutes until they are golden brown and their bases sound hollow when tapped with your fingertips. Leave to cool on a wire rack, then dust with icing sugar, if desired.

FIG & FENNEL RICOTTA BREAD
Pane ai fichi, finocchio e ricotta

This sweet flatbread with ricotta is from Tuscany. This recipe is flavoured with fennel seeds, but you could use walnuts, raisins or figs instead. Serve it for breakfast with homemade fig preserve – this is my favourite combination!

15 g/$\frac{1}{2}$ oz. fresh yeast, crumbled

225 ml/scant 1 cup body temperature water

1 x 125 g/$4\frac{1}{2}$ oz. tub of ricotta, at room temperature

2 teaspoons fine sea salt

100 g/$3\frac{1}{2}$ oz. dried figs, chopped

pinch of fennel seeds

500 g/$3\frac{1}{2}$ cups strong white flour, plus extra for dusting

2–3 tablespoons olive oil

1 large/US extra-large egg yolk

large baking sheet, greased

Serves 8–10

To make the dough, dissolve the yeast in some of the water in a large bowl. Stir in the ricotta, salt, dried figs and fennel seeds. Add the flour, little by little, using only enough to make a soft, pliable dough.

Turn the dough out onto a lightly floured work surface. Knead it for 10 minutes, incorporating more flour if necessary to keep the dough from sticking. The dough should be smooth and tender. Transfer it to a large bowl and drizzle and rub olive oil over it. Cover the bowl with a damp tea/dish towel and leave it for 1 hour, or until the dough has doubled in size.

When the dough is ready, knock it back, turn it out onto a lightly floured work surface and knead for 2 minutes. Flour the dough lightly and wrap in a clean tea/dish towel and rest for 5 minutes.

Preheat the oven to 200°C/180°C fan/400°F/Gas 6.

Flatten the dough with a rolling pin and shape it into an oval, roughly 33 x 20-cm/13 x 8-inch in size. Transfer the dough to the baking sheet. Cut an 18-cm/7-inch long slit lengthways through the centre of the dough, cutting all the way down to the baking sheet. Spread the split open slightly. Cover the dough with a damp tea towel and let it prove for 15 minutes.

Make the egg wash by beating the egg yolk with 1 tablespoon water in a small bowl. Brush the egg wash over the surface of the dough.

Bake the loaf on the centre shelf of the oven for 25–30 minutes or until it is rich brown and cooked through. Tap the bottom of the bread with your fingertips – it will sound hollow when it's done. Leave it to cool on a wire rack.

PEAR & ALMOND BREAD
Pane alle pere e mandorle

A wonderful combination of flavours, and particularly delicious when there is a glut of pears. A lovely and easy-to-make bread, with a deliciously soft crumb from the high milk content. I often serve this for breakfast to my students when in Italy, and it is usually requested more than once!

450 g/scant 3½ cups Italian 00 flour, plus extra for dusting
1 tablespoon fine sea salt
55 g/¼ cup caster/superfine sugar
85 g/scant 1 cup ground almonds
40 g/3 tablespoons unsalted butter, softened and diced
25 g/1 oz. fresh yeast, crumbled
300 ml/1¼ cups milk, warmed
2 ripe pears, peeled, cored and diced
125 g/1½ cups flaked almonds
75 g/2¾ oz. dark/bittersweet chocolate, melted (optional)

large baking sheet, greased

Serves 8–10

Mix the flour, salt, sugar and ground almonds in a large bowl and rub in the butter until the mixture resembles breadcrumbs. Make a well in the centre. Dissolve the yeast in a little of the milk and pour it into the well, along with the remaining milk. Mix to make a sticky dough.

Tip the dough out onto a lightly floured surface and knead it for 5 minutes until it is smooth and elastic. Place the dough in a lightly oiled bowl, cover with a damp tea/dish towel and leave to rise for 1 hour until it has doubled in size.

Knock back the dough, then knead it for 2–3 minutes on a lightly floured surface. Press the pears and half of the almonds on top of the bread, then knead until they are evenly distributed.

Flatten the dough into a round shape, then make deep cuts on the top in a criss-cross pattern. Scatter over the remaining almonds. Place the dough on the prepared baking sheet, cover with the damp tea towel and leave to prove for 1 hour, or until it has doubled in size.

Meanwhile, preheat the oven to 180°C/160°C fan/350°F/Gas 4.

Bake the loaf for 25–30 minutes until it has risen and is golden and the base of the bread sounds hollow when tapped with your fingertips. Leave to cool on a wire rack.

Use a spoon to drizzle the bread with melted chocolate, if using, before serving.

FLATBREAD WITH GRAPES
Schiacciata con l'uva

This sweet pizza is typical of Tuscany, where I first enjoyed it. Served with a dollop of mascarpone on the side, it is the Italian equivalent of an English cream tea. It is also good as a snack served with a glass of wine, or even with cheese.

350 g/2½ cups strong white flour, plus extra for dusting

pinch of fine sea salt

85 g/½ cup minus 1 tablespoon golden caster/superfine sugar

10 g/⅓ oz. fresh yeast, crumbled

150 ml/⅔ cup whole/full-fat milk, gently warmed

FILLING & TOPPING

200 g/1½ cups raisins

150 ml/⅔ cup vin santo or a sweet dessert wine

500 g/1 lb. 2 oz. black grapes (uva fragola if possible)

rosemary, finely chopped, to finish

large baking sheet, floured

Serves 8–12

Put the raisins for the filling in a bowl, pour over the wine and leave to soak for at least 2 hours. (You can do this the night before making the bread.)

Meanwhile, in a large bowl, mix the flour, salt and 55 g/¼ cup of the sugar and make a well in the centre. Cream the yeast with the warmed milk, then add this liquid to the well in the flour. Mix to form a soft dough.

Turn the dough out onto a lightly floured work surface and knead for 10 minutes until it is smooth. Put it in a bowl, cover with a damp tea/dish towel and leave in a warm place for 1 hour, or until it has doubled in size.

Knock the dough back and knead it again for 1–2 minutes on a lightly floured surface. Drain the raisins.

Divide the dough into two even pieces. Roll out each piece into a 24-cm/9½-inch round. Place one round on the prepared baking sheet and cover with half the grapes and half of the strained raisins. Dampen the edge of the dough and cover with the second round. Press to seal the edges together, using a little water if needed. Top with the remaining grapes and raisins. Cover and leave to prove in a warm place for about 20 minutes or until it is doubled in size.

Preheat the oven to 180°C/160°C fan/350°F/Gas 4.

Sprinkle the dough with the remaining sugar, then bake in the preheated oven for about 45 minutes until golden. Leave to cool slightly before serving warm, decorated with chopped rosemary.

SWEET PIZZA
Pizza dolce

This is a really delicious take on pizza. My grandmother used to make it as a *merenda* (snack) for after our siesta, and we accompanied it with a strong espresso – yes, even as children! My Nonna would give it to us with cream and we felt incredibly grown up. The bread base is topped with a creamy layer and then with fresh fruit. It's good for breakfast too. You can use your imagination and add further ingredients – try some grated or shaved chocolate on top and/or some toasted chopped hazelnuts.

BRIOCHE DOUGH

20 g/¾ oz. fresh yeast

175 ml/¾ cup milk, warmed

450 g/3¼ cups strong white flour

4 large/US extra-large eggs

2 large/US extra-large egg yolks, plus 1 extra to glaze

5 tablespoons golden granulated sugar

½ teaspoon salt

250 g/1 cup plus 2 tablespoons unsalted butter, softened, in pieces

CREAM CHEESE & FRUIT TOPPING

200 g/1 cup full-fat cream cheese

2 large/US extra-large egg yolks

2–3 drops of vanilla extract

1 tablespoon caster/superfine sugar

250 g/9 oz. fresh fruits (strawberries, raspberries, blueberries etc.)

STREUSEL TOPPING

175 g/scant 1 cup light soft brown sugar

25 g/3 tablespoons plain/all-purpose flour

50 g/3½ tablespoons unsalted butter, melted

grated zest of 1 orange

2 large baking sheets, lined

Makes 2–3 pizzas

To make the brioche: cream the yeast in the milk. Mix in 125 g/1 cup of the flour to make a sticky sponge or dough. Cover this with the rest of the flour but do not mix it in. Leave, covered, for 45 minutes in a warm place so the sponge bubbles up through the flour.

Mix the flour into the sponge. Add the whole eggs, yolks, sugar and salt and continue mixing until the dough is very elastic. Mix in the soft butter, bit by bit, waiting for it to be incorporated before the next addition. Knead for 5 minutes until the dough is smooth and elastic.

Cover and leave to rise overnight in the fridge. It should triple in size. If necessary, leave to rise further in the morning. Divide the dough into 2–3 pieces and roll out into flat circles, 5–8 mm/⅛ inch thick. Place on the prepared baking sheets, cover and set aside while you prepare the toppings.

Preheat the oven to 200°C/180°C fan/400°F/Gas 6.

To make the toppings, mix the cream cheese with the egg yolks, vanilla and sugar. Combine all the streusel topping ingredients together in a bowl.

Cover each brioche base with the cream cheese mix and top with fruits, then sprinkle over the streusel topping.

Glaze any visible brioche dough with the egg yolk glaze, then bake in the preheated oven for 25–30 minutes or until the crust is puffed and golden and the streusel topping is crunchy.

SMALL CAKES, PASTRIES & BISCUITS

Pasticcini e biscotti

Take delight in small bites

If some alcohol and a slice of cake might be a little much for me at breakfast, I wouldn't say no to an espresso accompanied by a small pastry or biscuit. *Pasticcerie* in Italy seem to specialize in small sweet things, in infinite varieties. In a bakery near where I teach in Puglia, displayed neatly in line, perfectly shaped, so enticing, are tiny doughnuts, miniature pastry parcels, multi-coloured amaretti, a plethora of variegated biscuits/cookies, and even little cakes formed from tiramisù.

Like bigger cakes and pastries, the smaller versions rely on similar flavourings and filling ingredients.

Perhaps the most common filling is a custard, of which there are many types in the Italian repertoire. One is a version of the French crème Anglaise, containing milk, egg yolks and sugar. This is the one for *zuppa Inglese*, with the added zing of lemon and vanilla. (And if cream were added, this could form the basis of a gelato.) Another Italian custard is a *crema pasticciera* (or the French *crème pâtissière*, also known as confectioners' custard), which is denser, using flour or cornflour as a thickener. This is used a lot in pancakes, in crisp pastries, in between cake layers, and in between a pastry case, large or small, and a filling of fruit. If you think about it, zabaglione is basically a type of custard.

Custard-making can be a temperamental business, primarily because of the effect of direct or too high heat on egg yolks. You don't want your custard to scramble! I would advise that you always use a proper double-boiler pan, or a heavy, heatproof mixing bowl that will happily sit on top of a saucepan containing

your hot water. The bottom of the bowl must not touch the water. Another tip is to always try to beat the egg yolks and sugar together first. Somehow the sugar helps prevent the egg yolks from scrambling when they meet heat – although the temperature must always be very low.

I give the basic *pasta frolla* recipe on page 54, and I use it here, but there are also a couple of other pastries – a choux and a puff, the latter used in my *cornetti* recipe (see page 115). The recipe is quite complicated, but mastering puff pastry is very empowering, I think! *Cornetti* always remind me of Milan, the widely acknowledged fashion centre of Italy. Its citizens are no less keen on sweet things than anywhere else in Italy, but when eating *cornetti*, they bend their elbows and eat the croissant from an angle, so that nothing drops on their beautiful clothes. In a Milan *pasticceria*, my daughter and I encountered about six people doing just that, and we could not help laughing!

Italians love biscuits, which they bake or buy for every day, or for special occasions: there are Christmas, Easter, All Saints' Day and St Valentine's Day specialities, all variously sweetened, spiced, shaped and decorated. The words 'biscuit' and *biscotto* both come from the same Latin root, rendered in French as *bis cuit*, which means 'twice baked'. The American word 'cookie' comes from the Dutch *koekje*, meaning 'little cake', introduced by Dutch settlers in the late 18th century. There are actually some Italian biscuits that are twice baked, usually the ones that are incredibly crisp, just begging to be dipped into a softening cappuccino or hot chocolate in the morning, or a vin santo in the evening.

Biscuits are the ideal present to take to friends. My students go home from their week's cooking course with a bag of my homemade biscuits: they are small, easy to eat, last well and are often packed with fruit and nuts, so are a good source of energy on long flights.

BLUEBERRY & LEMON DRIZZLE POLENTA CAKES

Torta di polenta al limone coi mirtilli

Italian blueberries are grown the length and breadth of Italy, but do substitute with other fruits if preferred. I have a life-long passion for polenta, I love it – not only for its texture, but for the cheerful bright yellow colour it brings to a cake. I make these at cookery classes for children and they are always well received.

125 g/½ cup plus 1 tablespoon/
 1⅛ sticks butter, softened
125 g/⅔ cup caster/superfine sugar
2 large/US extra-large eggs
100 g/⅔ cup fine polenta/cornmeal
 (not instant or quick cook)
 or semolina
25 g/3 tablespoons plain/
 all-purpose flour
1 teaspoon baking powder
pinch of salt
grated zest of 1 lemon
½ teaspoon vanilla extract
2–3 tablespoons milk
100 g/1 cup blueberries

FOR THE DRIZZLE
grated zest and juice of 1 lemon
60 g/¼ cup plus 2 teaspoons
 caster/superfine sugar

12-hole cupcake pan

Makes 12

Preheat the oven to 200°C/180°C fan/400°F/Gas 6. Either line the cupcake pan with paper cases or grease with butter and sprinkle with a little sugar.

In a large mixing bowl, cream the butter and sugar together until light and fluffy, then gradually beat in the eggs. Don't worry if the mixture curdles slightly.

In a separate bowl, combine the polenta, flour, baking powder and salt, then gently fold this into the batter. Fold in the lemon zest, vanilla and enough milk to give the batter a gentle, dropping consistency. Fold in roughly three-quarters of the blueberries.

Spoon the batter into the holes of the cupcake pan, press the remaining blueberries on top and bake for 20 minutes until golden and a skewer inserted into the middle of a cake comes out clean.

For the drizzle, mix together the lemon zest and juice and the sugar. Prick each cake a few times with the skewer and spoon over the lemon sugar mixture, then leave to cool in the pan.

Note: *These little cakes are delicious served with mascarpone or warm out of the oven with vanilla ice cream.*

SWEET RICOTTA PASTRIES
Soffioni abruzzesi

These small pastries are excellent for any time of the day. The traditional recipe is just flavoured with lemon but other inclusions such as Amarena cherries in syrup would be wonderful in the filling or on top once baked. Orange zest can be substituted for lemon, or even chocolate and nuts would work a treat.

½ quantity of Pasta Frolla dough (see page 54), plus extra flour for dusting

200 g/7 oz. ricotta

100 ml/scant ½ cup double/ heavy cream

100 g/½ cup caster/superfine sugar

2 large/US extra-large eggs, separated

grated zest of 1 lemon

few drops of vanilla extract

Amarena cherries, chocolate or hazelnuts, to serve (optional)

muffin mould with 7-cm/2¾-inch holes

Makes 6

Preheat the oven to 180°C/160°C fan/350°F/Gas 4.

Roll the pastry out on a lightly floured surface into an 11-cm/4½-inch square and cut into six even squares. Place each square in a hole of the muffin mould.

Whisk the ricotta, cream, sugar, egg yolks, lemon zest and vanilla extract together in a large bowl.

Whisk the egg whites in a separate bowl until light and fluffy, then incorporate into the ricotta mixture.

Spoon the mixture into the pastry lined muffin cases, folding the excess pastry around the filling.

Bake in the preheated oven for 30 minutes, then lower the temperature to 160°C/140°C fan/325°F/Gas 3 and cook for a further 10 minutes to crisp the pastry. Dust with icing sugar, if desired, and serve with cherries, chocolate or hazelnuts.

ITALIAN DOUGHNUTS
Bombolini

225 g/1⅔ cups strong white flour

15 g/½ oz. fresh yeast, dissolved in 75 ml/⅓ cup warm water

85 g/½ cup minus 1 tablespoon caster/superfine sugar

100 ml/scant ½ cup white wine

finely grated zest of 1 lemon

55 g/⅓ cup sultanas/golden raisins

sunflower oil, for frying

icing/confectioners' sugar, for dusting

Serves 4–6
(makes about 12)

Mix all the ingredients together, except for the oil and icing sugar, and beat well into a smooth batter. Let this rest for 1 hour in a warm (not hot) place.

Put a deep pan of sunflower oil on to heat and test the temperature by dribbling a little of the batter into it; if it sizzles and turns golden, the oil is ready.

Working in batches and using a teaspoon, drop the batter into the oil in spoonfuls, taking care not to overcrowd the pan, and cook for about 4 minutes until golden brown all over. Remove and drain well on paper towels. Serve hot with a light dusting of icing sugar.

These cakes are similar to doughnuts, and are truly wonderful. I often serve these for breakfast, or at any special family gathering with sparkling Prosecco.

CANNOLI
Cannoli

The literal meaning of *cannoli* is 'small tube' and the tiny pastry is also associated with Siciliana Carnevale as a fertility symbol. I've really tried my hardest with this recipe to deliver the ultimate *cannoli* and made many tweaks along the way. I've decided to make a larger number here, so you only fry once, and they will keep well in an airtight box. If they are not crisp enough, they can be popped in a hot oven for 10 minutes to get the desired crispiness. We all love *cannoli* so much and often have them for breakfast in Sicily. They can even be made as a sweet canapé for a party.

250 g/1¾ cups plus 2 tablespoons Italian 00 flour, plus extra for dusting

20 g/4 teaspoons caster/ superfine sugar

large pinch of bicarbonate of soda/ baking soda

1 teaspoon cocoa powder

pinch of salt

40 g/3 tablespoons unsalted butter

1 large/US extra-large egg yolk

30 ml/2 tablespoons dry Marsala

1 egg white, to seal

1 litre/4 cups sunflower oil

icing/confectioners' sugar, for dusting

FILLING

150 ml/⅔ cup double/heavy cream, whipped

300 g/10½ oz. strained ricotta

75 g/⅓ cup caster/superfine sugar

2 teaspoons vanilla extract

grated zest of 1 lemon

½ teaspoon ground cinnamon

OPTIONAL DECORATIONS

2 tablespoons finely chopped candied orange peel

2 teaspoons mini chocolate chips

2 tablespoons chopped pistachios

10½-cm/4-inch cookie cutter
28 cannoli moulds (see Note)
piping/pastry bag

Makes 28

Mix all the dry ingredients together and add the butter and rub into the flour mixture until it resembles breadrumbs. Add the egg yolk and Marsala and mix well until smooth, adding a little more flour if the mixture is too wet. Leave the dough covered in the fridge for 1 hour while you make the filling.

For the filling, whip the cream and add the strained ricotta, sugar, vanilla, lemon zest and cinnamon.

On a flour-dusted surface, roll out the dough to about 2mm/⅛ inch thin (this is very important to roll as thinly as you can), then use the cookie cutter to cut out 28 circles. Wrap each circle around a *cannoli* mould, using the egg white to seal.

Heat the oil in a deep saucepan or deep-fat fryer to 180°C/350°F. Working in batches, fry the dough wrapped around the *cannoli* moulds for 1 minute on each side until golden. Drain on kitchen paper and repeat for all of the *cannolis*.

Spoon the filling into a piping bag and pipe into each *cannoli*. Press the chocolate chips, pistachios or candid peel to the ends of the mixture, if liked. Dust with icing sugar, dive in and enjoy. When they are filled, they become a little soggy so they should be eaten as quickly as possible (and certainly within 1–2 hours).

Note: Cannoli *moulds can easily be bought online. These can also be cooked in batches if you don't have enough moulds.*

LEMON & VANILLA CREAM PASTRIES
Zeppole di San Giuseppe

I'm so happy to have this very special pastry in the book. It's usually enjoyed as part of celebrations for Father's Day in Italy.

60 g/¹/₄₄ cup/½ stick butter
60 g/¼ cup plus 2 teaspoons
   caster/superfine sugar
pinch of sea salt
300 g/2¼ cups Italian 00 flour
6 large/US extra-large eggs
vegetable oil, for deep frying
icing/confectioners' sugar,
   for dusting
Amarena cherries (or glacé
   or dried cherries), to top

LEMON & VANILLA CUSTARD
250 ml/1 cup milk
250 ml/1 cup extra thick double/
   heavy cream
finely grated zest
   of 1 lemon
1 vanilla pod/bean, split and
   seeds scraped
6 large/US extra-large egg yolks
140 g/scant ¾ cup caster/superfine
   sugar
50 g/heaping ⅓ cup Italian 00 flour

piping/pastry bag fitted with
   a large star nozzle/tip

Makes 16

For the lemon and vanilla custard, put the milk, cream, lemon zest and vanilla pod and scraped seeds into a saucepan and bring to just below the boil over a medium heat. Remove from the heat, then set aside for 20 minutes to infuse.

Whisk the egg yolks and sugar in a bowl until pale, add the flour and whisk to combine. Strain the milk mixture through a fine-mesh sieve/strainer, return to the heat and bring to just below the boil. Now, whisking continuously, pour a quarter of the milk mixture over the yolk mixture and whisk to combine. Add the remaining milk mixture, whisk to combine and transfer to a clean saucepan. Whisk continuously over a medium heat until the mixture comes to the boil, then cook, whisking continuously, for about 3–4 minutes until very thick. Remove from the heat, transfer to a large bowl, cover closely with cling film/plastic wrap and set aside to cool to room temperature.

For the pastry, bring the butter, sugar, a pinch of sea salt and 250 ml/1 cup water to a simmer in a saucepan over a medium heat. Add the flour, stir to combine, then cook, stirring, for 2–3 minutes until the mixture forms a smooth ball and pulls away from sides of the pan. Transfer to an electric mixer fitted with a paddle attachment. Beat on a low speed, adding the eggs one at a time and beating well between each addition. Transfer to the piping bag and set aside to rest for 20 minutes.

Heat the oil in a deep-fryer or deep saucepan to 180°C/350°F. Pipe the dough into 5-cm/2-inch diameter rings on small squares of baking paper. Carefully add the rings to the hot oil in batches, paper-side up, and deep-fry for 1–2 minutes until the rings loosen from the paper; be careful, hot oil will spit.

Carefully remove the paper from the oil with tongs and discard. Turn the rings and cook for 1–2 minutes until golden and puffed. Drain on paper towels and let cool to room temperature.

Pipe each zeppola with a little lemon and vanilla custard, dust with icing sugar, top with a cherry and serve.

BAKED SWEET PASTRIES
Minne di Sant'Agata

These dome-shaped pastries are made from a sweet pasta dough. Their shape has inspired the name which, when translated literally, means 'breasts of Saint Agatha'. There are regional variations, but this version is from Amalfi.

225 g/8 oz. plain/all-purpose or Italian 00 flour
65 g/¼ cup plus 1 tablespoon caster/superfine sugar
100 g/½ cup minus 1 tablespoon unsalted butter, cut into pieces
1 large/US extra-large egg
1 tablespoon finely grated unwaxed lemon zest
pinch of sea salt
icing/confectioners' sugar and cocoa powder, for dusting

FILLING
1 tablespoon toasted hazelnuts
1 tablespoon candied orange peel or mixed peel
25 g/1 oz. plain chocolate (50% cocoa solids)
225 g/8 oz. ricotta
55 g/¼ cup caster/superfine sugar
1½ teaspoons vanilla extract
1 large/US extra-large egg yolk

7.5-cm/3-inch cookie cutter

Makes 12

To make the pastry, put the flour and sugar into a food processor and, working on full speed, add the butter pieces gradually until well mixed. With the food processor still running, add the egg, lemon zest and salt. Turn the dough out onto greaseproof paper, flatten, cover and chill in the fridge for 30 minutes. Leave to come to room temperature before rolling.

For the filling, finely chop the hazelnuts and orange peel and grate the chocolate. Push the ricotta through a sieve/strainer into a bowl. Stir in the sugar, vanilla, egg yolk, orange peel, hazelnuts and chocolate until well mixed.

Preheat the oven to 180°C/160°C fan/350°F/Gas 4. Grease a large baking sheet.

Roll out the pastry until about 5 mm/¼ inch thick and use the cookie cutter to cut out about 24 circles. Put 2 teaspoons of the filling on half the pastry circles and top with the remaining pastry circles. Press to seal all round. Place on the baking sheet and make several slits across the top with a sharp knife.

Bake the small parcels in the preheated oven for about 20 minutes until golden. Leave to cool, then dust with icing sugar and cocoa powder to finish.

PASTICCIOTTO

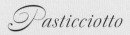

Pasticciotto

These are utterly divine served warm for breakfast as they do in Lecce.
They are quite rich, so I usually cut them in half to enjoy.

**1 quantity of Pasta Frolla dough
  (see page 54)**
**1 quantity of Lemon & Vanilla
  Custard (see page 99)**
**6 Amarena cherries in syrup
  (I use the ones from Fabbri),
  roughly chopped**
1 egg yolk, beaten, to glaze
**icing/confectioners' sugar,
  for dusting**

6 x pasticciotto moulds
  (oval non-stick 11-cm/4½-inch
  moulds, 3 cm/1¼ inch deep;
  they can be bought online)

Makes 6

Make the lemon and vanilla custard following the instructions on page 99. Cover and set aside to cool.

Preheat the oven to 180°C/160°C fan/350°F/Gas 4.

Roll out the pasta frolla on a flour-dusted surface, making sure it is not too thin, about 5mm/¼ inch. Upturn the mould on the pastry and cut out ovals big enough to line the moulds. Cut out six ovals for the lids.

Line the moulds, with some pastry overhanging, then almost fill the pastry cases/shells with the cooled custard. Spoon a teaspoon of the chopped cherries in syrup on top of the custard. Brush the edge of the pastry with egg yolk and top with the pastry lids. Press to seal the pastry lids in place, trim off any overhanging pastry leftover, then glaze the tops with beaten egg.

Place the filled moulds on a baking sheet and bake in the preheated oven for 25–30 minutes until they are golden. Enjoy as they are, or dusted with icing sugar.

Note: *You could also fill with pistachio cream (see page 158) or a chocolate cream for a different flavour.*

SPICED FIG BISCOTTI
Biscotti ai fichi

This spiced fig jam is unbelievably scrumptious, and particularly useful if you have a good crop of figs, but if you don't, fig jam is readily available and also excellent. I first enjoyed these biscotti when I was teaching in Puglia, many years ago.

185 g/³/₄ cup plus 1 tablespoon/
   1¹/₂ sticks softened butter
165 g/³/₄ cup plus 1 tablespoon
   caster/superfine sugar
2 large/US extra-large egg yolks
scraped seeds of 1 vanilla pod/bean
225 g/1³/₄ cups Italian 00 flour
60 g/²/₃ cup ground almonds
¹/₂ teaspoon baking powder

SPICED FIG JAM

1 vanilla pod/bean, split and
   seeds scraped
2 cinnamon sticks
thinly peeled zest and juice
   of 1 lemon
1 kg/2¹/₄ lb. black figs (about 10),
   trimmed and roughly chopped
400 g/2 cups golden caster/
   superfine sugar
1 teaspoon rose water (optional)

large baking sheet, lined with
   baking paper

Makes 12

First, make the spiced fig jam. Tie the split vanilla pod, cinnamon sticks and lemon rind in a piece of muslin/cheesecloth with kitchen string. Combine the vanilla seeds, remaining ingredients and muslin parcel in a saucepan with 200 ml/scant 1 cup water and stir occasionally over a medium heat until the sugar dissolves. Bring to the boil, then reduce the heat to low and stir occasionally, breaking up the figs gently with a wooden spoon, until the jam reaches setting point (place a spoonful of the jam on a saucer in the fridge for 10 minutes; if it wrinkles and sets, it is ready). Remove the muslin parcel and set the jam aside to cool before pouring into a sterilized jar, then seal.

Preheat the oven to 170°C/150°C fan/325°F/Gas 3.

Beat the butter, sugar, egg yolks and vanilla seeds in a stand mixer until pale. Mix the flour, ground almonds and baking powder in a separate bowl, then spoon in the beaten butter and sugar mixture. Stir to combine, then roll tablespoons of the mixture into balls and place 5 cm/2 inches apart on the prepared baking sheet. Gently flatten each biscotti slightly. Make a small indentation in the top of each biscotti, then fill the dip with a teaspoon of spiced fig jam.

Bake in the preheated oven for 30–35 minutes until golden. Set aside to cool slightly on the baking sheet, then serve warm with extra jam.

Note: *Spiced fig jam, unopened, will keep refrigerated for up to 3 months.*

CRUNCHY MINI MERINGUES
Brutti ma buoni

Ugly but so good, these are scrumptious and well worth making to be served
on the side of an espresso cup, or even given as gifts of food. When I tested the recipe
for this book I didn't have enough hazelnuts and used half hazelnuts and half pecans and I was
thrilled with the results. Doing a little research on this recipe, I discovered that they can
be made another way, cooked in a pan. However I quite boldly and confidently am proud
of this particular method. The traditional recipe calls for all hazelnuts.

200 g/1½ cups toasted hazelnuts
2 large/US extra-large egg whites,
    lightly beaten
pinch of sea salt
100 g/½ cup icing/confectioners'
    sugar
½ teaspoon vanilla extract
35 g/2 tablespoons caster/
    superfine sugar

2 large baking sheets, lined with
    baking paper

Makes 12–14

Preheat the oven to 120°C/110°C fan/250°F/Gas ½.

In a food processor, pulse the hazelnuts to grind them to a coarse crumb.

With an electric hand whisk, whisk the eggs with the salt until stiff peaks
form. Add the remaining ingredients and whisk again until thick and glossy.

Add 1 rounded teaspoon of the mixture to the lined baking sheets, spaced
slightly apart. Bake in the centre of the oven for 40–45 minutes until
golden. Leave to cool on a wire rack before serving.

TWICE BAKED COOKIES
Biscotti alle mandorle

275 g/2 cups plain/all-purpose
    or Italian 00 flour
150 g/¾ cup caster/superfine sugar
1 teaspoon baking powder
2 large/US extra-large eggs,
    plus 1 egg yolk
1 teaspoon vanilla extract
2 drops of almond extract
100 g/¾ cup unblanched whole
    almonds

large baking sheet, lined with
    baking paper

Makes 24

Preheat the oven to 180°C/160°C fan/350°F/Gas 4.

Place the flour, sugar, baking powder, eggs, egg yolk and vanilla and
almond extracts in a bowl and mix together well by hand. Add the
almonds and knead until mixed together to make a dough.

Divide the dough into six even pieces, then form each piece into a long
rectangle, flattening the top slightly.

Arrange on the prepared baking sheet and bake in the oven for about
20 minutes.

Remove from the oven and cut each biscuit at an angle into 2-cm/¾-inch
thick biscotti. Return to the oven for a further 10 minutes until golden.
Transfer to a wire rack and leave to cool.

These cookies are called *biscotti* in Italian. They are baked twice, which makes them dry and ideal for dipping into vin santo at the end of a meal. There are many variations, so you may want to experiment using hazelnuts instead of almonds. They are perfect enjoyed with a coffee.

CHOCOLATE ALMOND BISCUITS
Cricchignoli

A lovely recipe from Puglia – almond, chocolate and lemon is a winning combination.

200 g/1½ cups unblanched almonds, roughly chopped

250 g/1¼ cups golden caster/superfine sugar

1 tablespoon unsweetened cocoa powder

grated zest of 1 lemon

3 large/US extra-large egg whites

1 teaspoon lemon juice

large baking sheet, lined with baking paper

Makes 18

Preheat the oven to 170°C/150°C fan/325°F/Gas 3.

Mix the almonds with 200 g/1 cup of the sugar, the cocoa powder and lemon zest.

Whip the egg whites to stiff peaks with the lemon juice (reserving 1 tablespoon of the egg white for brushing later) and carefully fold into the almond mixture.

Dip your fingers in the bowl and, taking a little mixture at a time, mould into small rounds on the baking sheet. Lightly brush the top of each biscuit with the reserved egg white and sprinkle with the remaining sugar. Bake in the preheated oven for about 20 minutes until crisp and golden. Remove from the oven and leave to cool on a wire rack before serving. Store in a sealed box for up to 5 days.

FRIED PASTRY BITES
Cenci

Originating from Florence and eaten at celebrations, this is traditionally the first dessert that children would cook with grandmothers. For added deliciousness, grated citrus zests can be added, with rum too.

350 g/2⅔ cups Italian 00 flour, plus extra for dusting

3 large/US extra-large eggs, beaten

3 tablespoons olive oil

2 tablespoons white rum (optional)

2 teaspoons vanilla extract

pinch of salt

100 g/½ cup caster/superfine sugar

1 litre/4 cups groundnut oil

icing/confectioners' sugar, for dusting

fluted pastry wheel

Makes 12–14

Place the flour in a large bowl and make a well in the centre. Add the eggs, olive oil, rum (if using), vanilla, salt and sugar to the middle of the well and mix with a fork, slowly working outwards until all the ingredients are blended.

Knead the dough on a lightly floured surface for about 15 minutes until very smooth, then leave to rest, covered, for 1 hour.

Roll the dough through a pasta machine to the number seven (or by hand until it is 2 mm/⅛ inch thick) and cut into finger-width strips using a fluted pastry wheel.

Heat the groundnut oil to 180°C/350°F in a deep pan and fry the strips, one at a time until golden. Remove with a slotted spoon and place on a paper towel to drain. Dust with icing sugar. These are best enjoyed straightaway.

FUDGED ESPRESSO SHORTBREAD
Pasticcini

A glorious combination of chocolate and walnuts that couples beautifully with the bitter coffee. Using maple syrup gives a lovely fudgey texture.

100 g/½ cup minus 1 tablespoon/ 1 stick unsalted butter, softened
50 g/¼ cup light brown muscovado sugar
150 g/1 cup plus 2 tablespoons plain/all-purpose flour
1 tablespoon maple syrup
pinch of salt
50 g/1¾ oz. dark/bittersweet chocolate (70% cocoa solids), broken into pieces
1 teaspoon vegetable oil

ESPRESSO WALNUT TOPPING
175 g/1¼ cups walnuts
50 g/3½ tablespoons unsalted butter
150 g/¾ cup light brown muscovado sugar
1 tablespoon espresso powder
5 tablespoons maple syrup
1 tablespoon plain/all-purpose flour
2 large/US extra-large eggs

23-cm/9-inch square cake pan, greased and lined

Makes 16

Preheat the oven to 180°C/160°C fan/350°F/Gas 4.

In a large bowl, beat the butter and sugar with a wooden spoon until pale. Fold in the flour, maple syrup and a pinch of salt. Press into the pan, smooth the surface, prick with a fork and freeze for 10 minutes.

Meanwhile, toast the walnuts for the topping in the preheated oven for 8 minutes. Leave to cool, then roughly chop and set aside.

Bake the shortbread for 20 minutes until golden.

For the topping, melt the butter in a pan, then simmer for 3 minutes until the white solids turn golden and it smells toasty. Take the pan off the heat, then whisk in the remaining topping ingredients and stir in the toasted nuts. Pour onto the hot shortbread and bake for a further 30 minutes until risen and set. Leave to cool completely in the pan.

To decorate, melt the chocolate and oil in the microwave or in a bowl set over a pan of simmering water. Drizzle over the bake (there will be some leftover) and transfer to the fridge briefly for the chocolate to set, before cutting into bars or squares as preferred.

ITALIAN CROISSANTS
Cornetti

250 g/1¾ cups strong
   white flour
250 g/1¾ cups plus
   2 tablespoons Italian 00 flour,
   plus extra for dusting
1½ teaspoons fine sea salt
18 g/⅔ oz. fresh yeast
100 g/scant ½ cup whole/
   full-fat milk, plus extra
   for brushing
2 large/US extra-large eggs,
   lightly beaten
60 g/¼ cup unsalted butter,
   at room temperature
100 g/½ cup caster/
   superfine sugar
seeds scraped from 1 vanilla
   pod/bean
grated zest of 2 oranges
icing/confectioners' sugar,
   for dusting

FOR LAMINATING
250 g/1 cup plus 2 tablespoons
   unsalted butter, at room
   temperature

VANILLA SYRUP
100 g/½ cup caster/
   superfine sugar
½ vanilla pod/bean, split

2 large baking sheets, lined
   with baking paper

Makes 20

The day before, add both flours and the salt to the bowl of a stand mixer. Dissolve the yeast in the milk, whisk well and add it to the flour. Add 80 ml/⅓ cup water and the lightly beaten eggs. Knead at low speed for 10 minutes with the hook attachment. Add the butter, then the sugar, vanilla seeds and orange zest. Knead for 10 more minutes at low speed, until the butter has been completely incorporated. You should get a ball of smooth, elastic dough. Place the dough in a plastic bag that has enough space to allow the dough to double in size. Store it in the fridge for 24 hours.

Prepare the butter to laminate the croissants, so it can chill overnight. With the help of a rolling pin, spread the butter between two sheets of baking paper into a square about 5 mm/⅛ inch thick, as even as possible. Store it in the fridge.

The next day, place the dough on a well-floured surface. Roll it into a round slightly larger than the butter sheet. Place the butter in the centre of the dough and gently pull the four sides of the dough over the butter to close it inside, as if in an envelope. Seal the edges. With the help of the rolling pin and some flour, roll out the dough so that it triples its length, keeping the same width so you have a long rectangle of dough.

Now make a three-fold. Turn the dough 90 degrees so it sits horizontally in front of you. Mentally divide the dough into three equal parts and fold the right third to the middle then fold the left third over the top to cover the middle. Seal the edges by pinching the dough together. Rotate the dough 90 degrees and roll the dough out into a rectangular sheet, quadrupled in length, keeping the same width.

Now make a four-fold. Turn the dough 90 degrees so it sits horizontally in front of you and mentally divide the dough into four equal parts. Fold the two outer quarters onto the two middle quarters, then fold again in the centre to close the dough, like a book. Seal the edges by pinching the dough together. Wrap the dough in cling film/plastic wrap and let it rest in the fridge for about 1 hour.

After this time, remove the dough from the fridge and roll it into a 5-mm/¼-inch thick rectangular sheet. With a sharp knife or a pizza wheel, cut it into two long strips, then cut each strip into long and narrow triangles across the width of the strip. You should get 20 pieces. Starting from the base, roll each triangle to make a croissant, tucking the tip of the triangle under the *cornetti* so that it won't open while rising. Arrange the *cornetti* on the prepared baking sheets, keeping them well spaced. Let them rise in a warm place for about 2 hours, or until they have doubled in size.

Meanwhile, prepare the vanilla syrup. Pour 100 ml/scant ½ cup water into a small saucepan, add the sugar and split vanilla pod and bring to a simmer over a low heat. Simmer for 5–8 minutes until thick and slightly golden. Set aside.

Preheat the oven to 190°C/170°C fan/375°F/Gas 5. Brush the *cornetti* gently with milk, then bake for 15–17 minutes until golden brown. Once out of the oven, brush them with the vanilla syrup, then dust with icing sugar to serve.

DESSERTS

Dolci

Sweet heavenly desserts

As I have said many a time, most Italian meals end with fruit rather than with more complicated desserts. The latter are relatively modern – Italy has more of a cake and pastry culture – and have probably been popularized by restaurants. As a child, I remember only sliced oranges in syrup and *zuppa Inglese*.... But on special occasions, of which there are many in Italy, anything can happen. The *nonna* (grandmother) might produce any one of a number of classic desserts, some of which have become very well known around the world, such as panna cotta, *zabaglione* and tiramisù. (Interestingly, when we visited that bakery in Specchia mentioned in the introduction, I saw that they had won the world championship for tiramisù. A tiny bakery in a small village at the very end of the Italian heel, what are the odds!)

I have included only one fruit recipe in this chapter, but you will have seen that fruit features in many of the other recipes – in cakes, tarts, pastries and, of course, ice cream. Stuffed figs are a favourite of mine, but you could also stuff halved peaches (bake them with crumbled amaretti in the hollow where the stone was). You could wine-poach pears and serve them drizzled with melted chocolate. Peaches, figs and apricots can all be poached in a wine and citrus juice bath until just tender – wonderful with ice cream. As would be dried fruit: figs or apricots poached in vin santo, or good sultanas or raisins in a sweet white wine. (Presented in pretty little jars they would also make very good Christmas presents.) I have occasionally made a sort

of crème brûlée, using zabaglione as the 'custard' on top of a selection of suitable fruits. And there is nothing quite like a fresh fruit salad, a *macedonia*, which is popular in most Italian households.

The main ingredients of Italian desserts are soft cheeses – ricotta and mascarpone – sponge, cream, eggs, sugar, chocolate and coffee, nuts and alcohol, often Marsala. Mascarpone is a rich cheese made from double/heavy cream, while ricotta is much lighter, a by-product of cheese-making, made from the whey. The flavour of the latter depends on the source of the milk, whether sheep, cow, goat or water buffalo.... All would be lovely in the *cassata*, stuffed figs or as a pancake filling for the apostles' fingers (see page 133).

The Genoese sponge on page 47 is used as a base in a few recipes here, such as the *cassata* (see page 122), *zuccotto* (see page 126) and *zuppa Inglese* (see page 129). Cream is a uniting factor in many desserts in Italy, as is chocolate. But both have to be treated with respect. Whipping double cream is easy if you have a machine, but you must be careful not to over-whip, as the cream can soon become too grainy and thick (remember that the end result of long-whipped cream is butter!). To rescue over-whipped cream, gently whip in a couple more tablespoons of cream, and that should solve the problem.

Melting chocolate is another potential disaster area. I prefer good dark chocolate, with 70 per cent cocoa solids, as this melts well, but other chocolates can be used. Professionals use chocolate drops rather than block chocolate. But if you are using the latter, chop it up into small even pieces, and place in a heatproof bowl over a pan of gently simmering water. The bowl must not touch the water. Allow to melt slowly, stirring regularly (continuously if using milk or white chocolate); you don't want the chocolate to 'seize'. Leave to cool a little once melted, then use. Often chocolate is melted with the addition of some butter or alcohol, which is much less potentially hazardous. And I have heard that you can melt chocolate in the microwave...

CLASSIC TIRAMISÙ
Tiramisù nel bicchiere

Literally translated this means 'pick me up', as the sugar and liquor lift the spirits. Make in a large serving dish or in individual portions - when presented in small glasses, they look very impressive!

6 large/US extra-large eggs, separated

100 g/½ cup caster/superfine sugar

200 ml/scant 1 cup double/ heavy cream

250 g/generous 1 cup mascarpone

200 ml/scant 1 cup freshly brewed espresso coffee

100 ml/scant ½ cup Marsala

24 savoiardi biscuits or sponge fingers

cocoa powder, for dusting

10–12 individual glasses or a 25-cm/10-inch serving dish

Serves 10–12

Beat the egg yolks and sugar together until light and fluffy in a bowl using an electric whisk. Using the same whisk, in another bowl, whip the cream to firm peaks, then add the mascarpone and just briefly whisk again to combine. Now use a hand whisk to briefly mix this into the egg yolk mixture until combined.

Whisk the egg whites to soft peaks in a clean dry bowl, then using a metal spoon or a whisk, mix into the cream mixture, incorporating as much air as possible.

Pour the espresso and Marsala into a large bowl ready for dipping the biscuits.

Cover the base of the glasses or serving dish with a 2-cm/ ¾-inch layer of the cream, then a layer of the biscuits that have been dipped quickly into the espresso mixture. You have to do the soaking and layering as you go or they'll become too soggy and traditionally Italians do not like soggy biscuits.

Continue to build the layers of cream and biscuits, ending with a layer of cream. Chill in the fridge, ideally for 6–24 hours. Dust with cocoa powder to serve.

SICILIAN CASSATA
Cassata Siciliana

This is a simple, classic dessert, made from ricotta and sponge cake, and should not be confused with *cassata gelata*, which is an ice-cream bombe. Prepare it a day ahead of time.

450 g/1 lb. ricotta

225 g/1 cup plus 2 tablespoons caster/superfine sugar

225 g/8 oz. dark/bittersweet chocolate (70% cocoa solids)

1 tablespoon ground cinnamon

2 tablespoons amaretto

175 g/6 oz. shelled pistachio nuts, chopped

200 g/7 oz. glacé fruits, chopped

12 savoiardi biscuits or sponge fingers

½ portion of Genoese Sponge Cake (see page 47), cut horizontally

TOPPING

225 ml/scant 1 cup double/ heavy cream

1 tablespoon amaretto

glacé fruit, to decorate

1.7-litre/3-pint pudding basin

Serves 8–10

Line the base and sides of the pudding basin with cling film/plastic wrap.

Beat together the ricotta and sugar until light and fluffy. Divide the mixture in half.

Chop half of the chocolate into small pieces. Add to one-half of the ricotta mixture with the cinnamon and amaretto. Fold the pistachio nuts and glacé fruits through the other half. Cover both mixtures and set aside.

Use the savoiardi biscuits to line the prepared bowl, pressing them firmly around the bowl so that they are even. Fill with the fruit ricotta mixture, then the chocolate ricotta mixture. Cover the top with the cake. Cover the bowl and freeze for 2 hours or longer.

Melt the remaining chocolate and pour over the top of the sponge in the bowl. Return to the freezer for about 15 minutes, until set.

To make the topping, whip the cream and amaretto together until it just holds its shape.

Just before serving, turn out the cassata. Run around the edge with a palette knife, then place a serving plate over the top. Invert the bowl onto the plate, and let the cassata gently ease out, chocolate-side down. Remove the cling film, then spread over the cream mixture to cover, and decorate with glacé fruit.

CARAMEL & CHOCOLATE DESSERT
Il bonet piemontese

This is a classic recipe from Piedmont – caramel, chocolate and amaretti – with many variations. It's elegant, and I love to serve it at dinner parties.

4 large/US extra-large eggs, plus 1 egg yolk

150 g/¾ cup caster/superfine sugar

35 g/⅓ cup unsweetened cocoa powder

pinch of salt

200 g/7 oz. amaretti cookies, crumbled, plus a few extra

2 tablespoons amaretto

500 ml/2 cups whole/full-fat milk

bite-size amaretti cookies, to serve

CARAMEL

150 g/¾ cup caster/superfine sugar

50 ml/scant ¼ cup water

25 x 11-cm/10 x 4½-inch loaf pan

Serves 8–10

Preheat the oven to 160°C/140°C fan/325°F/Gas 3.

Make the caramel by adding the sugar and water to a pan, stir to dissolve, then bring to the boil. When it turns a caramel colour, leave to cool, then pour into the loaf pan.

Mix the whole eggs and egg yolk in a bowl, then add the sugar and gently mix together until smooth (no whisking!). Sift in the cocoa powder and salt. Stir to incorporate, then add the crumbled amaretti cookies and amaretto. Slowly pour in the milk and mix until well combined.

Pour the mixture into the pan on top of the caramel. Place the pan in a deep roasting pan and pour water so that it comes halfway up the side of the pan (a bain-marie). Bake in the preheated oven for 60 minutes. Unmould, slice or scoop onto serving plates and serve with amaretti cookies.

LEMON MARSCAPONE CHEESECAKE
Cheesecake al limone

This popular dessert is very easy to make. It can be made with ricotta instead of mascarpone if you wish, and can be served with fresh strawberries or raspberries when they are in season.

85 g/3 oz. unsalted butter

175 g/6 oz. amaretti cookies, crushed

400 g/14 oz. mascarpone

finely grated zest of 3 lemons and juice of 1, plus pared zest of 1 lemon, to decorate

115 g/4 oz. caster/superfine sugar

2 large/US extra-large eggs, separated

2 tablespoons cornflour/cornstarch

pinch of salt

edible flowers, to decorate

deep 20-cm/8-inch loose-bottomed cake pan, base and sides well buttered

Serves 8

Preheat the oven to 180°C/160°C fan/350°F/Gas 4. Melt the butter. Mix the amaretti crumbs into the melted butter and press into the bottom of the prepared cake pan.

Put the mascarpone, lemon zest and juice, sugar and egg yolks in a bowl and, using a wooden spoon, mix together. Sprinkle the cornflour over the top and fold in.

In a separate bowl, whisk the egg whites with the salt until stiff. Fold into the cheese mixture. Spread the mixture into the cake pan and smooth the top. Bake for 35 minutes until firm to the touch. Leave to cool in the pan.

Decorate with lemon zest and edible flowers.

Illustrated on page 6

TUSCAN TRIFLE
Zuccotto

This traditional Tuscan trifle, which translates to English as 'little pumpkin', is recognized by the classic pattern on the icing sugar and cocoa decoration. It is particularly good when served the day after it's made. Keep in the fridge until served.

oil, for greasing

140 g/5 oz. dark/bittersweet chocolate (70% cocoa solids)

45 g/⅓ cup blanched almonds, toasted

45 g/⅓ cup blanched hazelnuts, toasted

1 litre/4 cups whipping cream

140 g/1 cup icing/confectioners' sugar

½ Genoise Sponge Cake (see page 47), cut horizontally

1 tablespoon each of rum, brandy and cherry brandy

2 tablespoons cocoa powder

fresh berries and grated chocolate, to decorate

1.7-litre/3-pint pudding basin

Serves 10–12

Line the base of the pudding basin with a circle of non-stick baking paper and lightly grease with oil.

Break half of the chocolate into a heatproof bowl and set the bowl over a saucepan of simmering water. Heat until melted, then remove the bowl from the heat. Chop the remaining chocolate into small pieces.

Roughly chop the almonds and hazelnuts. Whip the cream until it holds its shape, then mix in the chopped nuts and chopped chocolate.

Divide the cream in half, then add the melted chocolate to one half and mix until combined. Sift 55 g/⅓ cup of the icing sugar into each half of the cream and stir in gently. Chill both creams in the fridge until required.

Slice the crust off the top of the cake half. Push the cake into the bowl and ease it up to line the sides.

Mix together the rum, brandy and cherry brandy. Brush the cake with the rum mixture to moisten it completely and help it to fit the bowl firmly. Trim off any untidy edges and use your hands to get as smooth a finish as you can.

Spoon in the white cream mixture and spread it evenly up the sides. Fill the centre with the chocolate mixture and smooth the top. Cover and place in the fridge for at least 2 hours before serving.

Cut out a circle of baking paper about the same size as the zuccotto will be when turned out. Draw even wedges onto the paper and cut out every other wedge, keeping the paper attached in the centre to create a stencil for decorating.

Turn the zuccotto out onto a serving plate. Sift the remaining icing sugar over the whole top. Place the cut-out paper over the top and liberally sift the cocoa over. Carefully remove the paper and you will have adorned the zuccotto with its classic design.

Serve decorated with fresh berries and grated chocolate.

ANCIENT ROMAN TRIFLE
Zuppa Inglese

This name is mysterious; it means 'English soup'. The name is said to honour Admiral Nelson's defeat of Napoleon's fleet at Abukir. Whatever the origin, *zuppa Inglese* has been popular in Rome for the last two centuries. In my research, there are countless variations, but this one really is a firm favourite with my whole family.

3 large/US extra-large eggs

115 g/½ cup plus 1 tablespoon caster/superfine sugar

115 g/¾ cup plus 2 tablespoons Italian 00 flour

½ teaspoon baking powder

3 tablespoons dry Marsala

300 ml/1¼ cups whipping cream

50 g/½ cup toasted flaked almonds, to decorate

CRÈME ANGLAISE

450 ml/scant 2 cups whole/full-fat milk

4 large/US extra-large egg yolks

85 g/scant ½ cup caster/superfine sugar

½ teaspoon salt

1 teaspoon vanilla extract

finely grated zest of 1 lemon

20-cm/8-inch springform cake pan, base and sides well buttered

Serves 10–12

Preheat the oven to 180°C/160°C fan/350°F/Gas 4.

Beat together the eggs and sugar for 10–15 minutes until thick and creamy. Sift the flour and baking powder together, then, using a metal spoon, fold into the egg mixture. Pour the mixture into the prepared pan and bake in the oven for 20 minutes until the cake is golden and has shrunk away from the sides of the pan. Leave to cool in the pan.

When cool, remove from the pan and place the cake in a large, heatproof serving bowl or individual serving dishes. Pour over the Marsala, break up the cake a little and set aside.

Meanwhile, prepare the crème Anglaise. In a saucepan, bring the milk to just below boiling point and keep it hot. In a bowl, whisk together the egg yolks, sugar and salt until pale and fluffy. Pour in the hot milk, stirring with a wooden spoon. Return the mixture to a clean pan and heat gently, stirring all the time, until the mixture thickens and coats the back of a wooden spoon. Stir in the vanilla extract and lemon zest and pour over the cake. Leave until cold.

When cold, whip the cream until it holds its shape, then use to cover the crème Anglaise. Scatter over the almonds to decorate.

PANNA COTTA
Panna cotta

Panna cotta means 'cooked cream', and it can be enjoyed in so many ways, from varying degrees of wobbliness to myriad shapes and flavours. I have opted for individual desserts in small moulds. However, do bear in mind that it can be made in a loaf shape, which cuts well when serving for a crowd and looks very elegant. This recipe can also be halved with ease.

140 g/scant ¾ cup caster/superfine sugar

435 ml/1¾ cups whole/full-fat milk

5 sheets of gelatine

500 ml/2 cups double/heavy cream

110 g/¾ cup icing/confectioners' sugar

2 tablespoons rum

1 tablespoon dry Marsala

2 teaspoons vanilla extract

TO SERVE

crushed toasted hazelnuts

chocolate shavings

whipped cream (optional)

8–10 individual moulds or ramekins (or a 23 x 12.5-cm/9 x 5-inch loaf pan)

Serves 8–10

Warm the moulds or loaf pan in the oven preheated to its lowest temperature, 120°C/100°C fan/250°F/Gas ½.

Heat the sugar in a small saucepan over a medium heat. Do not stir until the sugar begins to melt around the edges, then stir with a wooden spoon until the sugar dissolves into a smooth syrup that is nutty brown in colour.

Quickly pour the caramel into the warm moulds or pan, then lift and rotate them to evenly coat the inside before the caramel sets and hardens.

Pour 60 ml/¼ cup of the milk into a small bowl, add the gelatine and leave to soften for about 2–3 minutes.

Scald the remaining milk, then remove the pan from the heat and add the gelatine mixture. Stir to dissolve completely.

In another saucepan, combine the cream with the icing sugar and warm to a medium heat. Do not boil! Stir constantly until the sugar is completely dissolved. Pour the cream mixture into a bowl and combine with the milk mixture, then leave to cool.

When cool, stir in the rum, marsala and vanilla extract. Pour through a fine-mesh sieve/strainer into the caramel-coated moulds or pan. Refrigerate for several hours until firm.

Turn the individual panna cottas out on to serving plates (or turn out from the loaf pan and cut into slices) and serve topped with crushed toasted hazelnuts, chocolate shavings and any of the syrup from the mould drizzled over the top.

Notes: *The addition of a little whipped cream on the side if liked is also wonderful.*

The dessert will unmould very easily if kept cold.

THE APOSTLES' FINGERS

Dita degli apostoli

Please don't be put off by the title! These fingers are carefully rolled pancakes
with a fresh ricotta and chocolate filling. When they have been cut,
they really do resemble fingers. Another Puglianese classic.
Quite unusual, but really delicious.

5 large/US extra-large eggs

25 g/2 tablespoons caster/
superfine sugar

125 g/1 cup plain/all-purpose
or Italian 00 flour

pinch of salt

225 ml/scant 1 cup milk

unsalted butter, for greasing

FILLING

450 g/1 lb. ricotta

175 g/scant 1 cup caster/
superfine sugar

grated zest of 1 lemon

grated zest of 1 orange

grated zest of 1 clementine
(optional), plus extra to decorate

1 tablespoon double/heavy cream

50 g/2 oz. dark/bittersweet
chocolate (70% cocoa solids),
plus extra to decorate

2 tablespoons rum

heavy 28-cm/11-inch non-stick
crêpe pan

Serves 8–10

To prepare the batter, whisk together the eggs and sugar until
well blended. Beat in the flour, add the salt and gradually add the
milk, whisking vigorously until the batter is smooth. Cover and
leave to stand for 30–60 minutes.

To make the filling, put the ricotta cheese into a bowl and beat in
the sugar, the zests and the cream until smooth. Finely chop the
chocolate and beat into the mixture with the rum.

Wipe the crêpe pan with a little butter and place over a medium
heat. When the pan is medium hot, ladle in enough batter to
cover the base. Cook until it bubbles and the underside is golden
brown, then turn and cook the other side until golden brown.
Remove from the pan and stack on a large plate, interleaved
with greaseproof paper. Repeat with the remaining batter to
make eight pancakes.

Lay a pancake on a work surface and cut away any brittle edges.
Place a heaped tablespoon of filling in the middle, then spread
very thinly over the whole pancake. Roll the pancake tightly
towards you. Repeat with each pancake.

Slice each rolled pancake at a slight diagonal into finger-length
pieces, discarding the ends of each roll. Chill in the fridge before
serving. If wished, decorate with orange zest and grated
chocolate and eat with your fingers.

STUFFED FIGS

Fichi farciti

The memory of picking figs straight from the trees as a child in Italy gives these fruits a sort of magic for me. I used to run home with armfuls of them, passing hundreds more squashed in the road. There are so many wonderful ways to eat figs, but of all the recipes, this is my favourite.

12 ripe fresh figs

55 g/2 oz. walnut halves, freshly shelled if possible, roughly chopped

3 tablespoons fragrant honey

3 tablespoons sweet red Italian vermouth

115 g/4 oz. mascarpone

100 g/3½ oz. dark/bittersweet chocolate (75% cocoa solids)

Serves 6

Preheat the oven to 200°C/180°C fan/400°F/Gas 6.

Cut a tiny slice off the bottom of each fig so that it will sit upright. Make two cuts down through the tops of the figs, about 2.5 cm/1 inch deep, at right angles, and ease the figs open.

In a bowl, mix together the walnuts, honey, vermouth and mascarpone. Spoon into the opened-out fig cavities, then place the figs in a baking dish. Bake in the preheated oven for 10–15 minutes.

Melt the chocolate in a bowl set over a pan of simmering water. Place the figs on a serving plate and drizzle with the melted chocolate to finish.

ZABAGLIONE

Zabaione

One of the reasons I'm married to my husband – this was made and relished by a guest at a dinner party my sister was hosting, who then became my boyfriend, and later husband! It is fantastic served over poached seasonal fruit and something you can whip together quickly and easily for a special dessert.

4 large/US extra-large egg yolks

4 tablespoons caster/ superfine sugar

3–4 tablespoons dry Marsala

fresh fruit, to serve (optional)

Serves 4

Beat together the egg yolks, sugar and Marsala in a glass bowl until light and airy.

Set the bowl over a saucepan of simmering water and cook, whisking continuously with an electric whisk.

Continue to whisk, keeping an eye on the temperature so the eggs don't coagulate, until very much increased in volume and light and fluffy, about 10 minutes.

Pour into serving glasses, possibly over some fresh fruit, and serve immediately.

ICE CREAM
& SORBETS
Gelati, semifreddi e sorbetti

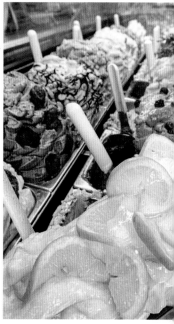

Ever popular frozen delights

Italy is famed and loved throughout the world for her *gelati* or ice creams. The Italians appreciate them just as much, especially during their steamy summers, when the cold freshness of a *granita*, *sorbetto* or *semifreddo* (various types of *gelati*) offers some relief from the relentless heat. (*Gelato*, the singular form, translates literally as 'iced' or 'frozen'.)

No one truly knows where, when and how ice creams came into being. Marco Polo is rumoured to have brought the idea back to Italy from China – but it is actually debatable whether he even visited that far-off country. The Arabs could have been influential: they ruled Sicily for some 200 years, and since then Sicily has played a major role in the history of ice cream, and produces some of the best. The Arabs are credited

with mixing ice from Mount Etna with fruit flavourings and fruit purées, but it could equally have been the Greeks or Romans – details are obscure.... But it was undoubtedly a Sicilian, one Francesco Procopio dei Coltelli, who opened a shop in Paris selling coffee and water ices in the late 17th century. That 'shop', Procope – café, restaurant and gelatier – is still trading in Paris, and still offering ice creams, sorbets and sundaes over 300 years later!

The first ices would have been water based, what we call water ices, or *sorbetti* and *granite*. The water-ice ingredients – water, flavourings, fruit purées etc. – were put in a bowl inside another container which contained salt mixed with ice. Salt reduces the freezing point of water and ice, and thus really low temperatures – low enough to freeze the water-ice ingredients – could be achieved. The mixture being frozen would have been hand-stirred, to break the coarse ice crystals up into smaller, smoother and more palatable pieces. Later, a basic *sorbetière* was used, which had

a handle that turned the mixture — much easier! As knowledge grew, different ingredients began to be added to the basic water-ice mixture: sweeteners such as honey or sugar, or fats such as milk, cream and eggs. All of these interfere with the way water freezes, and actually slow down the crystallization process, which makes the finished result smoother and softer. Alcohol too has a low freezing point, which makes a boozy ice-cream softer. And vigorous stirring or churning, latterly with electricity of course (our modern ice-cream machines), meant that air was incorporated into the ice cream, which softens the mixture further.

Italian *gelati* are smoother and cleaner in taste than most other ice creams, because they contain less fat: fat (such as in milk or cream) coats the tongue, interfering with one's ability to taste. Typically, an American cream ice might have well over ten per cent fat, whereas an Italian one could contain considerably less than ten per cent. Italian *gelati* are also churned

more slowly than other cream ices, which means less air is introduced, making the finished product denser and much softer in texture.

Gelati are usually served at slightly warmer temperatures than British or American ice creams. Semifreddo is an ice cream which is soft, like a cross between a parfait and a mousse, its name meaning literally 'half frozen'; it is not normally churned. Other Italian cream ices include *spumoni* (a moulded iced dessert), and *cassata* (a Sicilian speciality, which uses the ingredients of a cake with the same name, such as marzipan and dried fruit).

One of my favourite things to do in Italy is stand in front of a *gelateria*, gazing at the jewel-like *gelato* choices in their individual containers. One should be enough, in a cone or dish, but often I might try two.... In Specchia last year, I had both chocolate and pistachio in a cone, which I ate using another tiny little cone as a scoop, rather than licking. A lovely touch — and the *gelati* were lovely too!

BITTER CHOCOLATE ICE CREAM
Gelato al cioccolato amaro

A grown-up version of Italy's favourite flavour.

8 large/US extra-large egg yolks

175 g/scant 1 cup golden caster/
  superfine sugar

1 litre/4 cups milk

200 g/7 oz. dark/bittersweet
  chocolate (70% cocoa solids),
  broken into pieces

250 g/2½ cups cocoa powder

ice-cream machine (optional)

Serves 12
(makes 1.5 litres/6 cups)

Whisk the egg yolks and sugar with electric beaters until very thick and pale.

Pour the milk into a saucepan, add the chocolate and cocoa and bring to a simmer, stirring constantly, until blended. Pour this over the yolk mixture while still hot, beating all the time.

Pour the chocolate mix into an ice-cream machine and churn until frozen following the manufacturer's instructions. Alternatively, pour the mixture into a container, freeze for 2–3 hours until beginning to firm up, then whisk thoroughly to break up any ice crystals before freezing again until solid. Leave to soften in the fridge for 20–30 minutes before serving.

PLUM ICE CREAM
Gelato alla prugne

This ice cream also works well with other members of the plum family, such as damsons or greengages.

450 g/1 lb. ripe plums, stoned/
  pitted and quartered

125 g/²⁄₃ cup light muscovado sugar

4 large/US extra-large egg yolks

125 g/¾ cup icing/confectioners'
  sugar

300 ml/1¼ cups double/heavy cream

2 tablespoons iced water

ice-cream machine (optional)

Serves 8
(makes 1 litre/4 cups)

Put the plums into a pan with the muscovado sugar and 300 ml/1¼ cups water. Bring to the boil, cover and simmer for about 10 minutes until the plums are really tender. Press the stewed fruit through a sieve/strainer. Chill the purée in the fridge for about 20 minutes.

Put the egg yolks and icing sugar in a bowl and set the bowl over a saucepan of gently simmering water, making sure the base of the bowl doesn't touch the water. Whisk with electric beaters until the mixture has just warmed through. Take the bowl off the heat and continue whisking until the mix has doubled in volume. Chill in the fridge.

Whip the cream with the iced water in a bowl until it just holds its shape. Add the plum purée and egg mixture and whisk lightly together.

Churn in an ice-cream machine following the manufacturer's instructions. Alternatively, pour the mixture into a container and freeze for about 1 hour until mushy. Turn into a chilled bowl and whisk vigorously. Return to the container and freeze for 2–3 hours until firm.

PEACH CREMOLATA
Cremolata di pesche

This is a lovely simple dish of frozen, crushed fruit pulp that is
served with unsweetened whipped cream. There is no need to add sugar
(unless the fruit isn't ripe), you don't need any fancy equipment and,
if you omit the cream, there's no fat involved either.

10 peaches, ultra-ripe ones,
 peeled, stoned/pitted
 and sliced
1 tablespoon caster/superfine
 sugar (optional)
150 ml/²/₃ cup double/
 heavy cream

Serves 6

Put the peaches into a large bowl. Taste them for sweetness
and sprinkle over some sugar if you think they need a little extra
sweetness. Crush the fruit to a pulp with a fork or a potato masher.

Put the bowl into the freezer for 45 minutes, then take it out, stir and
crush the fruit again. Return the bowl to the freezer for 20 minutes
at a time, repeating the stirring and crushing until the crushed fruit
looks and feels like sherbet, which will take about 1–1½ hours.

Softly whip the cream. Scoop the cremolata into bowls and top with
whipped cream to serve.

Note: *Please put your serving vessel in the freezer, to keep the
cremolata frozen when served.*

RASPBERRY GRANITA
Granita al lampone

There are so many delicious, refreshing water ices or granitas in Italy,
but raspberries make a particularly good one.

grated zest and juice of
 1 lemon
700 g/4½ cups raspberries
150 g/³/₄ cup granulated sugar

ice-cream machine (optional)

Serves 6

Put all the ingredients into a saucepan and heat gently until the
sugar has dissolved, then simmer gently for 10 minutes. Take off
the heat, sieve/strain and leave to cool.

Pour into an ice-cream machine and churn until frozen following
the manufacturer's instructions. Alternatively, pour into a shallow
container and freeze for about 1 hour until ice crystals start to form.
Put the mixture into a chilled bowl, and using a fork, break up the
ice crystals. Return to the freezer for a further 2 hours or until firm.
Transfer to the fridge for 30 minutes before serving to soften.

SEMIFREDDO WITH CARAMEL FIGS

Semifreddo ai fichi caramellati

Semifreddo means 'semi-cold', so your serving vessel should be frozen
for best results. This is a very pretty dish with a celebratory feel and gives a great
impression at a dinner party.

6 large/US extra-large
  egg yolks
80 g/⅓ cup caster/
  superfine sugar
185 ml/¾ cup dry Marsala
grated zest of 1 lemon
½ teaspoon vanilla extract
375 ml/1½ cups double/
  heavy cream, lightly
  whipped

CARAMEL FIGS
230 g/generous 1 cup
  caster/superfine sugar
6 figs, halved

20 x 11-cm/8 x 4½-inch
  loaf pan
baking sheet lined with
  baking paper

Serves 6–8

Place the egg yolks, sugar, Marsala, lemon zest
and vanilla in a heatproof bowl over a saucepan of
simmering water, making sure the bowl does not
touch the water. Whisk for 5–6 minutes or until
the mixture is fluffy and almost doubled in volume.
Remove from the heat and leave to cool, whisking
occasionally. Fold in the cream, then pour into
the loaf pan. Freeze for 4 hours.

Meanwhile, make the caramel figs. Put the sugar
and 80 ml/⅓ cup water into a small saucepan and
place over a medium-high heat, swirling (not stirring!)
the pan gently until the caramel is golden. Remove
from the heat.

Using a fork, dip the fig halves into the caramel,
making sure they are coated evenly. Be very careful
as the caramel is extremely hot. Place the figs on the
prepared baking sheet, leave the caramel to harden for
10 minutes. Don't refrigerate as the toffee will soften.

Remove the semifreddo from the freezer, leave for
5 minutes, then turn out onto a platter. Serve in slices
with the caramel figs.

ZABAGLIONE ICE CREAM
Gelato allo zabaione

The other reason why I'm married (see page 134). I was cooking at a dinner party for my sister, where my husband was in attendance. He fell in love with this ice cream, and me!

4 large/US extra-large egg yolks

125 g/⅔ cup golden caster/superfine sugar

150 ml/⅔ cup dry Marsala

150 ml/⅔ cup whipping cream

Serves 4

Put the egg yolks into a large heatproof bowl that will fit over a saucepan. Add the sugar and whisk until the mixture is pale and thick and leaves a trail when the beaters are lifted.

Whisk in the Marsala, then set the bowl over a pan of simmering water, making sure the base of the bowl doesn't touch the water, and continue whisking until the mixture has at least doubled in volume.

Remove from the heat, stand the bowl in cold water and whisk until cool.

Whip the cream until it just holds its shape. Add to the cold zabaglione and whisk together. Pour into a container and freeze for about 1½–2 hours, or until firm. Serve in small bowls or glasses.

RICE ICE CREAM
Gelato di riso

You might be alarmed by the inclusion of ground rice here, but please try it, you will be amazed. The texture of the rice gives this ice cream body and substance. This is a particular favourite of mine, and I first enjoyed it at a famous *gelateria* in Rome. You can serve the ice cream with seasonal fruits or a chocolate sauce.

250 g/9 oz. ground rice

pinch of sea salt

grated zest of 2 lemons

1 litre/4 cups whole/full-fat milk

8 large/US extra-large eggs, separated

300 g/1½ cups caster/superfine sugar

500 g/2¼ cups mascarpone

2 teaspoons vanilla extract

250 g/9 oz. crushed amaretti biscuits, plus extra to decorate

fresh cherries, to serve

ice-cream machine (optional)

Serves 4

Put the ground rice in a saucepan with the salt, lemon zest and milk. Cook over a low heat for 25 minutes, stirring occasionally, until the mixture is thick and smooth. Leave to cool.

Beat the egg yolks with the sugar until pale and creamy. Add the mascarpone cheese and mix thoroughly.

Whisk the egg whites until peaks form, then add the vanilla. Fold the mascarpone mixture into the egg whites gently but thoroughly. Fold in the rice mixture along with the crushed amaretti.

Pour into an ice-cream machine and churn following the manufacturers' instructions. Alternatively, pour into a shallow freezer container and freeze for 2 hours. Serve in small bowls or glasses topped with crushed amaretti and cherries, if liked.

BLOOD ORANGE & CAMPARI SORBET

Sorbetto all'arancia rossa con Campari

I love this incredibly glamorous dessert. A wonderful combination
of flavours, not only good to drink, but also as a sorbet.

500 ml/generous 2 cups
blood orange juice (from
about 6 blood oranges)
125 g/²/₃ cup caster/superfine
sugar
100 g/3½ oz. liquid glucose
4 tablespoons Campari
juice of 1 lemon

ice-cream machine (optional)

Serves 4–6

Put the blood orange juice and sugar into a saucepan and warm
over a gentle heat, stirring until the sugar has dissolved. Add the
glucose, remove from the heat and stir again until dissolved. Pour
in the Campari and lemon juice. Transfer to a metal bowl and leave
to cool, then chill.

Churn in an ice-cream machine following the manufacturer's
instructions, then firm up in the freezer. Alternatively, put the bowl in
the freezer for 1–2 hours until the edges start to freeze. Whisk into the
centre, then freeze again. Repeat every hour for the next 2–3 hours
until the sorbet is smooth. Return to the freezer to firm up.

Serve in small bowls or glasses that have been chilled in the freezer
for 1 hour beforehand. The alcohol means it will melt quickly.

WATERMELON SORBET

Sorbetto all'anguria

The amount of sugar used in this recipe can be varied depending on the sweetness
of the watermelon. During the long hot summers in Italy, when people are prostrate
with heat, a spoonful of this delicious sorbet can revive them.

1 watermelon, cut into wedges
and seeds removed
golden caster/superfine sugar,
to taste

ice-cream machine (optional)

Serves 4

Remove the skin from the watermelon and cut the flesh into
chunks. Purée in a food processor until smooth. Add the sugar,
a couple of tablespoons at a time, until it is sweet enough.
Remember that the cold will dull the flavours a little.

Chill the purée for 2 hours, then churn in an ice-cream machine
following the manufacturer's instructions. Alternatively, pour into
a shallow container and freeze for 1 hour until ice crystals start to
form. Put the mixture into a chilled bowl, and using a fork, break
up the ice crystals. Return to the freezer for a further 2 hours or
until firm. Store the sorbet in the freezer until ready to serve.

VODKA LEMON ICED DRINK
Sgroppino al limone

This is something I always look forward to diving into, usually at the end of a busy week of teaching in Italy. It provides refreshment, cheer and utter deliciousness that you can never forget.

6 scoops lemon sorbet,
    preferably homemade
    (see below) or shop-bought
100 ml/scant ½ cup vodka
    (that has been kept in the
    freezer, so well chilled)
2 glasses of chilled good-quality
    Prosecco or sparkling wine

LEMON SORBET (SERVES 6)
175 g/scant 1 cup granulated sugar
8 large unwaxed lemons

ice-cream machine (optional)

Serves 4

Place four glasses in the freezer well beforehand. (I use tall champagne or wide, cup-shape glasses.)

Make the lemon sorbet first, if using homemade. Make a sugar syrup by putting the sugar in a saucepan with 450 ml/scant 2 cups water and gently heating until it dissolves. Bring to the boil, then gently boil for 10 minutes without stirring.

Meanwhile, using a potato peeler, peel the zest from the lemons and add to the sugar syrup. Leave to infuse until the syrup is cold.

Squeeze 440 ml/scant 2 cups juice from the lemons and pour into a mixing jug. Strain the cold syrup, stir in the lemon juice and mix well together.

Pour into an ice-cream machine and freeze following the manufacturer's instructions. Alternatively, pour into a shallow freezer container, cover and freeze for about 1 hour until mushy in texture. Remove from the freezer and tip the frozen mixture into a bowl. Beat well with a fork to break down the ice crystals. Return to the freezer container and freeze for a further 2 hours, or until firm.

For the iced drink, put the sorbet, vodka and Prosecco or wine into a blender and blend until you get a firm and frothy consistency. Scoop into glasses and serve with spoons.

Notes: *For the best results you should use a blender and make sure all of the ingredients and the bowl/jug are very cold, including the glasses in which they are to be served.*

If serving the lemon sorbet on it's own, decorate with lemon slices if liked.

EDIBLE GIFTS

Regali

A gift for all seasons

In Britain, you might take a bottle of wine or box of chocolates to a dinner party in someone's house; in the USA, you might take part of an entire course, for a pot-luck supper, say. In Italy, things are much more casual. Italians love to *passatiempo*, 'pass the time', and are very informal about popping into each others' houses, for coffee in the morning or afternoon, or for a drink in the evening. It is rare that they would arrive empty handed, and will almost always bring something edible as a gift for the host, which will often be homemade, and more often that not, will be something sweet.

On a daily basis, biscuits/cookies would be the ideal gift. Many of the biscuits here would be a great accompaniment to coffee or tea (or alcohol). Most are traditional Italian mixtures and shapes, but you can alter the look of your biscuits. Think of making a heart shape for Valentine's Day, or a ball shape for a sports-mad birthday boy. Use your imagination!

Whole cakes and tarts, large or small, as well as sweet breads, make good gifts too. A harassed Christmas or Easter Day host might be delighted if you offered to bring an Italian cake. It would save them a lot of time, and would be lighter than a traditional fruit cake. You could offer to bring something to a finger-food party: the apostles' fingers (see page 33) would be perfect as a 'dessert', as they are small and easy to eat by hand. (If you place a flaked almond at one end of each finger, it will look like a nail – for a Hallowe'en party perhaps?) And I think the American idea of

pot-luck – sharing the cooking of a lunch, supper or dinner – is a great one: an Italian tart, carefully packaged, perhaps alongside a frozen container of homemade ice cream, would be very happily received. But remember to discuss all this in advance: these sorts of offering cannot be spur of the moment!

The sweets in this chapter are ideal gifts, especially the candied fruit (my sisters often get this at Christmas, along with other treats). But all of these gifts need to be presented in suitable packaging, to keep them from breaking or spoiling, or simply to make them look more beautiful. For an informal occasion, take biscuits in a freezer box or other plastic container or bag. For a more formal present, wrap biscuits individually in tissue paper – like the commercial amaretti – and place in a pretty box or jar. I re-use empty and thoroughly cleaned coffee and passata jars, but Kilner or Mason jars would be good, come in many sizes, and are not

too expensive to buy. I like the idea of the 'double' donation: something to eat as well as a container that will be useful later.

Let your imagination fly when thinking of how to package your gifts: you can buy attractive plastic and cellophane bags – tie them with ribbon – and pretty cardboard boxes, some with transparent tops. I have used cleaned-out cans, which I cover with paper, and top with cellophane. (I actually use cans as a baking container, see the panettone recipe on page 173). You can even buy edible wrapping paper! And don't forget to add a little label or tag, either to identify the gift (and how to use or keep it if necessary), or the giver or receiver.

I love the concept of an edible gift that is homemade: someone has spent time and energy making something to give someone else pleasure. It's the ultimate token of friendship, of love even.

ALMOND, HAZELNUT & PISTACHIO TORRONE

Torrone al pistacchio, mandorla e nocciola

I have had a lifelong obsession with *torrone*. It's not hard work to make and delivers a really reliable result, so makes the perfect edible gift. A must-have piece of equipment to make this perfectly every time, is a sugar/candy thermometer.

2–4 sheets of edible rice paper

150 g/generous 1 cup whole almonds

100 g/²/₃ cup shelled unsalted pistachios

50 g/¹/₃ cup hazelnuts

2 large/US extra-large egg whites

300 g/1¹/₂ cups caster/superfine sugar

1 teaspoon vanilla extract

pinch of salt

250 g/scant 1 cup fragrant honey

50 g/3 tablespoons liquid glucose

¹/₄ teaspoon cream of tartare

20-cm/8-inch square baking pan, greased with neutral oil and lined with baking paper

sugar/candy thermometer

Makes 30–40 pieces

Preheat the oven to 180°C/160°C fan/350°F/Gas 4.

Cover the base of the prepared baking pan with a single layer of the rice paper, it may need to be trimmed to fit in the pan exactly. Set aside.

Tip all the nuts onto a baking sheet and lightly roast in the oven for about 4–5 minutes, then roughly chop once cooled.

Place the egg whites with 1 tablespoon of the sugar, the vanilla extract and salt into a bowl or a free-standing mixer with a whisk attachment and leave to one side for the moment.

Warm the honey in a small saucepan over a low heat until just boiling. Remove from the heat and keep warm.

Tip the remaining caster sugar, liquid glucose, cream of tartare and 75 ml/¹/₃ cup water into another pan and stir gently over a low heat to dissolve the sugar. Pop the sugar thermometer into the pan, bring the syrup to the boil and continue to cook until it reaches 149°C/300°F. Remove the pan from the heat, carefully add the hot honey, stir well, return to the heat and continue to cook until the syrup returns to 149°C/300°F.

Slide the pan off the heat and, working quickly, whisk the egg whites on a fast speed until stiff peaks form. Reduce the speed of the mixer slightly and gently pour the hot honey syrup onto the egg whites in a slow steady stream, whisking constantly. The mixture will foam up dramatically as the hot syrup cooks the egg whites. Increase the speed to medium and continue to whisk for another 3 minutes until the mixture is very thick and a pale buttermilk colour. Fold in the chopped nuts using a rubber spatula.

Quickly scoop the mixture into the prepared pan and spread into a smooth, even layer using a palette knife. Press a single layer of rice paper on top of the *torrone*, flatten completely using another baking pan and weigh the top down with a couple of cans. Leave to cool overnight.

The next day, when the *torrone* is completely cold, turn it out of the pan and onto a chopping board. Peel off the baking paper and, using a greased kitchen knife, cut into strips or squares to serve.

Note: *You can cut this delicious* torrone *into bars, wrap in cellophane and finish with some decadent ribbon for a delicious gift.*

PISTACHIO MERINGUES
Meringhe al pistacchio

Meringues always remind me of Mummy. She made these with elegant ease for us to devour, and often served them at parties sandwiched together with cream.

4 large/US extra-large egg whites

pinch of cream of tartare

110 g/½ cup plus 2 teaspoons caster/superfine sugar

110 g/¾ cup plus ½ tablespoon icing/confectioners' sugar

3 tablespoons chopped pistachios

¼ teaspoon rose water (optional)

1 teaspoon grated orange zest

Pistachio Cream (see below), to serve (optional)

2 large baking sheets, lined with baking paper

Makes 10

Preheat the oven to 140°C/120°C fan/275°F/Gas 1.

Place the egg whites in a large bowl, add the cream of tartar and whisk until stiff peaks form. Add a spoonful of the caster sugar and whisk again. Continue to do this, a few spoonfuls at a time, whisking after each addition.

Now do the same with the icing sugar, working quickly so you don't lose volume and you end up with a stiff, shiny mixture.

Finally, whisk 2 tablespoons of the pistachios, the rose water and the orange zest in to the meringue mixture quickly.

Spoon the mixture onto the prepared baking sheets, adding about 2 generous tablespoons per meringue. Sprinkle the tops with the remaining pistachios, reduce the oven temperature to 120°C/110°C fan/250°F/Gas ½ and bake for 45 minutes. Leave the meringues in the oven until they are cold with the door ajar. Serve with the pistachio cream, if liked.

PISTACHIO CREAM
Crema dolce di pistacchio

This Sicilian speciality can be enjoyed in so many ways: added to whipped cream as a filling for profiteroles, in tarts or pies, and quite simply on toast. I also love it in tiny half moon pastries for breakfast with a strong espresso.

200 g/2 cups raw unsalted pistachios

150 g/5½ oz. white chocolate, broken into pieces

100 ml/scant ½ cup double/ heavy cream

Makes a 200-g/7-oz. jar

Soak the pistachios in warm water for 20 minutes. Drain, then leave to cool.

Melt the white chocolate in a heatproof bowl over a pan of hot water, then leave to cool.

Place the nuts, chocolate and cream in a food processor and blend until bright green, luscious and smooth. Decant into a jar and store in the fridge for up to 2 weeks.

AMARETTI MOMBARUZZO
Amaretti (ricoperti al cioccolato)

I first enjoyed these as a shop-bought cookie, then had to find out more about them and learn how to make them myself as they were so delicious. They are from the Piedmont region in Italy and are absolutely delicious.

2 large/US extra-large egg whites

100 g/1 cup ground almonds (freshly and finely ground for max flavour)

120 g/½ cup plus 4 teaspoons golden caster/superfine sugar

grated zest of 1 lemon

2 drops of natural almond extract

TOPPING

50 g/1¾ oz. dark/bittersweet chocolate

1 teaspoon unsalted butter

large baking sheet, lined with baking paper

Makes 14

Preheat the oven to 190°C/170°C fan/375°F/Gas 5.

With a handheld whisk or in a stand mixer, whisk the egg whites until firm peaks form.

Add the ground almonds, sugar, lemon zest and almond extract and mix on a low speed until well incorporated.

Divide the mixture into conker-sized balls, each about 30 g/1 oz. and place on the prepared baking sheet. Bake in the preheated oven for 13 minutes until golden. Leave to cool on a wire rack until cold.

Melt the chocolate and butter in a heatproof bowl set over a pan of simmering water. Half-dip the Amaretti in the melted chocolate and leave to set. Enjoy with an espresso.

ALMOND & PISTACHIO BISCOTTI
Biscotti con mandorle e pistacchi

100 g/½ cup minus 1 tablespoon/ 1 stick minus 1 tablespoon butter

100 g/½ cup caster/superfine sugar

210 g/1½ cups Italian 00 flour, plus extra for dusting

60 g/½ cup shelled raw pistachios, finely ground

60 g/½ cup blanched almonds, finely ground

1 vanilla pod/bean, seeds scraped out

grated zest of 1 lemon

icing/confectioners' sugar, for dusting

2 large baking sheets, lined with baking paper

Makes 24

Preheat the oven to 180°C/160°C fan/350°F/Gas 4. Melt 2 tablespoons of the butter and use it to brush over the lined baking sheets.

Beat the remaining butter and sugar in an electric mixer until light and fluffy. Add the flour, ground nuts, vanilla seeds and lemon zest, then beat on a low speed until it all comes together. Turn out the mixture and knead to form a dough.

Dust your hands with flour and divide the dough into 24 pieces. Roll each piece into a ball in your palms and divide the balls between the lined baking sheets, spacing them apart.

Bake in the preheated oven for 15 minutes until lightly golden. Leave on a wire rack to cool, then dust with icing sugar to serve.

Anything with a pistachio always feels so glamorous, and the combination of the two nuts here is quite delicious. Package these little treats in pretty boxes or bags for the perfect gift.

ALMOND & HAZELNUT AMARETTI
Amaretti alle nocciole e mandorle

These are one of my most requested recipes, which originates from my friend Lucy's mother. Enjoy with an espresso or ideal packaged as a pretty gift.

2 large/US extra-large egg whites

100 g/1 cup freshly ground hazelnuts

100 g/1 cup freshly ground almonds

185 g/1¼ cups icing/confectioners' sugar, plus extra for dusting and shaping

1 teaspoon baking powder

1 teaspoon grated lemon zest

handful of flaked almonds, to decorate

2 large baking sheets, lined with baking paper

Makes 12

Preheat the oven to 160°C/140°C fan/325°F/Gas 3.

Whisk the egg whites in a clean bowl to form soft peaks. Add all the remaining ingredients, except the flaked almonds, to the egg whites and mix well.

Place a small amount of icing sugar for dusting into a shallow bowl. Use a dessertspoon to drop a spoonful of dough into the icing sugar, roll to coat all over and flatten with your hands.

Decorate the amaretti with some flaked almonds and place on the prepared baking sheet. Repeat until the mixture has been used up. Bake for about 20 minutes until lightly golden brown. Cool on a wire rack and dust with more icing sugar, if liked, then devour.

FLORENTINES
Florentine

115 g/scant 1 cup whole blanched almonds

115 g/scant 1 cup whole blanched hazelnuts

115 g/scant 1 cup shelled Brazil nuts

225 g/8 oz. natural glacé cherries

115 g/4 oz. glacé fruits, such as lemon, orange, pineapple or papaya

55 g/3½ tablespoons plain/all-purpose or Italian 00 flour

½ teaspoon ground allspice

½ teaspoon freshly grated nutmeg

115 g/generous ½ cup caster/superfine sugar

115 g/⅓ cup honey

55 g/2 oz. dark/bittersweet chocolate (70% cocoa solids)

23-cm/9-inch cake pan, greased and lined

Makes 12 wedges

Preheat the oven to 180°C/160°C fan/350°F/Gas 4.

Put the almonds, hazelnuts and Brazil nuts on a baking sheet and roast for 8–10 minutes. Tip the nuts into a mixing bowl and leave to cool. Wash and dry the cherries and glacé fruits and add to the nuts.

Sift the flour, allspice and nutmeg over the glacé fruits and mix well.

In a saucepan, warm the sugar and honey together over a low heat until the sugar has dissolved. Add the honey mixture to the fruit and stir.

Turn the mixture into the prepared pan and level the top. Bake for 25–30 minutes, then leave to cool in the pan.

Break the chocolate into pieces and melt it in a heatproof bowl set over a pan of boiling water. Drizzle or spread over the nut mixture in an even layer. When cold, cut into wedges and serve.

Florentines are ideal for sharing with friends who pop round for coffee, and they make good presents if wrapped attractively.

CHOCOLATE & HAZELNUT COOKIES

Baci di dama

The use of potato flour will give you the lightest, melt-in-the mouth texture to these iconic cookies. Hailing from Piedmont, where the finest hazelnuts are grown, *baci di dama* translates to 'lady's kiss'.

100 g/³/₄ cup blanched hazelnuts, toasted

100 g/¹/₂ cup unsalted butter

100 g/¹/₂ cup golden caster/ superfine sugar

100 g/³/₄ cup potato flour or Italian 00 flour

pinch of salt

1 teaspoon vanilla extract

80 g/3 oz. dark/bittersweet chocolate

large baking sheet, lined with baking paper

Makes 12

In a food processor, grind the hazelnuts to fine flour. Add the butter and sugar and blend again. Sift in the flour and salt and add the vanilla. Pulse gently to bring together into a dough, then chill for at least 1½ hours.

Preheat the oven to 180°C/160°C fan/350°F/Gas 4.

Use a teaspoon to make balls of the mixture and place them on the prepared baking sheet. Bake for 15 minutes until golden brown, then transfer to a wire rack to cool.

For the filling, heat the chocolate in a heatproof bowl set over a pan of simmering water until melted. Spread a small spoonful of chocolate on half of the cooled biscuits. Leave to set for 10–15 minutes, then sandwich another biscuit on top of each. Serve with coffee.

CHOCOLATE SALAMI

Salame di cioccolato

This is a rather special chocolate and biscuit mixture. It is easy to make, and goes beautifully with coffee at the end of a meal. Take it as a gift when you go to eat with friends.

125 g/1 cup mixed nuts, including pistachios

150 g/5¹/₂ oz. petit beurre biscuits

225 g/8 oz. dark/bittersweet chocolate (70% cocoa solids)

75 g/¹/₃ cup/³/₄ stick unsalted butter

2 tablespoons brandy

25 g/2 tablespoons ground almonds

1 large/US extra-large egg, plus 1 egg yolk

cocoa powder, for dusting

Makes about 20 slices

Spread the mixed nuts evenly in a grill/broiler pan and grill for 2–3 minutes, shaking the pan frequently until the nuts are golden. Finely grind the nuts in a food processor, then transfer to a bowl.

Chop the biscuits in the food processor until roughly crushed and place in a second bowl.

Break the chocolate into pieces and put in a small saucepan. Cut the butter into small pieces, add to the chocolate with the brandy and heat gently until melted. Pour the melted chocolate mixture into the bowl of crushed biscuits. Add the ground almonds and mixed nuts, egg and egg yolk and mix together. Leave the mixture in the fridge for about 2 hours, or if short of time, place in the freezer for 20 minutes, until it is solid.

Turn the chocolate mixture onto a piece of baking paper and shape into a sausage about 23 cm/9 inches long. Put the roll back in the fridge until ready to serve. Dust with sifted cocoa powder and cut up into slices as thick or as thin as you wish.

CANDIED PEEL
Scorze di candite

While researching this recipe, I came across literally hundreds of recipes and variations. I asked family, friends and Sicilian relatives and I've ended up with this recipe, which works really well. Sicilian *candite* is extremely diverse, with all sorts of fruits and flavours used.

1 orange
1 lemon
1 grapefruit
350 g/1¾ cups caster/
    granulated sugar

1 vanilla pod/bean,
    split lengthways
1 star anise
1 cinnamon stick

Makes 200 g/7 oz.

Using a sharp knife, cut the orange into four wedges and remove the flesh. Cut each piece of peel into three or four chunky strips. Repeat with the lemon and the grapefruit.

Place the peels into a saucepan, cover with cold water and bring to the boil. Simmer for 10 minutes, then drain. Repeat this process twice more as it removes the bitterness. Drain the peels and set aside while you prepare the sugar syrup.

Tip the sugar into a heavy-based pan and add 350 ml/ 1½ cups water. Add the vanilla, star anise and cinnamon. Place over a medium heat to dissolve the sugar, stirring occasionally.

Add the peels to the pan and boil steadily for about 40 minutes, stirring occasionally, until the peels become soft and translucent, and almost all of the syrup has been absorbed. Keep a close eye as it cooks as the syrup can burn.

Using tongs, remove the peels from the pan one at a time and lay on a sheet of baking paper in a single layer. Cover and leave to dry overnight. They should no longer be sticky. Store in a box or airtight container for up to 1 month.

Note: *You can chop the peel and add to cakes, biscuits, cookies and desserts or package and give as a wonderful gift, especially at Christmas.*

PANETTONE

Panettone

Panettone comes from Milan in northern Italy. The breads are exported
in attractive tall boxes, which can be seen hanging in Italian delicatessens
all over the world. Panettone made at home is not as tall as the commercial
varieties, and the texture is not quite so open, but it makes a deliciously
light alternative to heavy Christmas cakes.

4 teaspoons fresh yeast
  (or 2½ teaspoons dried yeast)
225 ml/scant 1 cup hand-hot milk
350 g/2⅔ cups plain/all-purpose
  or Italian 00 flour, plus extra
  for dusting
100 g/½ cup minus 1 tablespoon/
  1 stick unsalted butter, softened
3 large/US extra-large egg yolks
50 g/¼ cup caster/superfine sugar
85 g/3 oz. chopped candied peel
  (see page 170)
50 g/⅓ cup sultanas/golden raisins
1 teaspoon grated nutmeg
icing/confectioners' sugar,
  for dusting

3 x 400-g/14-oz. empty food cans
  (opened with a can opener, paper
  labels removed, ensure there are
  no dents in the can and that they
  are well washed) or a baking pan
  or dish of a similar size

**Makes 3 small
panettone** (Serves 9)

Grease the insides of the three clean cans. Cut strips of baking
paper, each measuring 55 x 33 cm/22 x 13 inches. Fold each
piece in half lengthways, then use it to line the cans. Line the
bases with a circle of baking paper, cut to size.

Blend the fresh yeast with 2 tablespoons of the milk until smooth,
then stir in the remaining milk. If using dried yeast, sprinkle it into
the milk. Leave in a warm place for 15 minutes until frothy.

Sift the flour into a large bowl and make a well in the centre.
Pour the yeast liquid into the well and, using a wooden spoon,
gradually draw in the flour from the sides of the bowl until well
mixed. Knead on a lightly floured work surface for 10 minutes
until smooth. Form into a ball and place in a lightly oiled bowl.
Cover with a clean tea/dish towel and leave to rise in a warm
place for 45 minutes, or until doubled in size.

Knead the softened butter into the dough with two of the egg
yolks, the sugar, candied peel, sultanas and nutmeg. Cover and
leave to stand, again in a warm place, for a further 45 minutes,
or until doubled in size.

Divide the dough into three pieces and knead each piece for
2–3 minutes. Form each piece into a smooth ball and place inside
the lined cans. Leave in a warm place for about 30 minutes, or
until risen to the top of the cans.

Meanwhile, preheat the oven to 200°C/180°C fan/400°F/Gas 6.

Brush the remaining egg yolk over the top of the doughs. Bake
in the preheated oven for 20 minutes, then lower the temperature
to 180°C/160°C fan/350°F/Gas 4 and bake for 20 minutes, or until
a skewer inserted in the centre comes out clean. Leave to cool in
the cans. Dust with icing sugar before serving.

The panettone can be stored in an airtight container for up to
a week.

INDEX

A

almonds: almond & hazelnut
amaretti 165
  almond & pistachio
    biscotti 161
  almond, hazelnut &
    pistachio torrone 157
  amaretti mombaruzzo 161
  blood orange & almond
    cake 29–30
  chocolate almond biscuits
    111
  Florentines 165–7
  pear & almond bread 80
  sticky plum, hazelnut &
    almond tart 54
  Tuscan trifle 126
  twice baked cookies
    107–8
amaretti biscuits: almond &
    hazelnut amaretti 165
  amaretti mombaruzzo 161
  caramel & chocolate
    dessert 125
  fig, amaretti & ricotta tart 73
  lemon mascarpone
    cheesecake 125
ancient Roman trifle 129
the Apostles' fingers 133
apples: apple vanilla cake
    with thick vanilla custard
    37
  Umbrian strudel 55

B

berries: very berry tart 69
birthday cake, Italian 34
biscotti: almond & pistachio
    biscotti 161
  spiced fig biscotti 104
biscuits: chocolate almond
    biscuits 111
  fudged espresso
    shortbread 112
  spiced fig biscotti 104
bitter chocolate ice cream
    140
blackberry & chocolate tart
    70
blueberry & lemon drizzle
    polenta cakes 91
Brazil nuts: Florentines
    165–7
brioche: sweet pizza 82
buns, mini cream-filled 74

C

cake pans, lining 8
cakes 10–47
  apple vanilla cake with
    thick vanilla custard 37
  blood orange & almond
    cake 29–30
  blueberry & lemon drizzle
    polenta cakes 91
  cappuccino loaf cake 44
  cherry & ricotta cake 15
  chestnut, chocolate &
    hazelnut cake 17
  chocolate sin cake 22
  fragrant coffee &
    cinnamon loaf cake 21
  Genoese sponge cake 47
  hazelnut & carrot cake 16
  hazelnut cake 33
  Italian birthday cake 34
  Italian doughnuts 92–4
  Italian plum cake 47
  peach & pistachio slice 43
  raspberry, orange, lemon
    & yogurt cake 38
  rhubarb, rosemary &
    pistachio strudel cake
    26
  rosemary & orange honey
    cake 38–40
  spiced pear & walnut cake
    22–4
  strawberry cake 29
Campari: blood orange &
    Campari sorbet 148
candied peel 170
  panettone 173
cannoli 96
cappuccino loaf cake 44
caramel: caramel &
    chocolate dessert 125
  semifreddo with caramel
    figs 144
carrots: hazelnut & carrot
    cake 16
cassata, Sicilian 122
cheesecake, lemon
    mascarpone 125
cherry & ricotta cake 15
chestnut, chocolate &
    hazelnut cake 17
chocolate: amaretti
    mombaruzzo 161
  the Apostles' fingers 133
  bitter chocolate ice cream
    140
  blackberry & chocolate
    tart 70

caramel & chocolate
    dessert 125
chestnut, chocolate &
    hazelnut cake 17
chocolate & hazelnut
    cookies 169
chocolate & pear tart 65
chocolate almond biscuits
    111
chocolate salami 169
chocolate sin cake 22
Florentines 165–7
fudged espresso
    shortbread 112
Italian birthday cake 34
pistachio cream 158
Sicilian cassata 122
stuffed figs 134
Tuscan trifle 126
cinnamon: fragrant coffee &
    cinnamon loaf cake 21
citrus fruit: candied peel 170
coffee: cappuccino loaf cake
    44
  classic tiramisù 121
  fragrant coffee &
    cinnamon loaf cake 21
  fudged espresso
    shortbread 112
compote, apple vanilla 37
cookies: chocolate &
    hazelnut cookies 169
  twice baked cookies
    107–8
cream: ancient Roman trifle
    129
  cannoli 96
  classic tiramisù 121
  lemon & vanilla cream
    pastries 99
  mini cream-filled buns
    74
  panna cotta 130
  pistachio cream 158
  semifreddo with caramel
    figs 144
  Sicilian cassata 122
  zabaglione ice cream 147
cream cheese: sweet pizza
    82
crema, hazelnut 66
crème Anglaise 129
cremolata, peach 143
croissants, Italian 115
crostata, fig & grape, with
    hazelnut crema 66
crunchy mini meringues 107
custard, vanilla 37

D

desserts 116–35
doughnuts, Italian 92–4
drink, vodka lemon iced 151

E

eggs: classic tiramisù 121
  pistachio meringues 158
  rice ice cream 147
  zabaglione 134
  zabaglione ice cream 147
equipment 8
espresso: fudged espresso
    shortbread 112

F

fennel seeds: fig & fennel
    ricotta bread 78
figs: fig, amaretti & ricotta
    tart 73
  fig & fennel ricotta bread
    78
  fig & grape crostata with
    hazelnut crema 66
  semifreddo with caramel
    figs 144
  spiced fig biscotti 104
  stuffed figs 134
  Umbrian strudel 55
flatbread with grapes 81
Florentines 165–7
fragrant coffee & cinnamon
    loaf cake 21
fruit: individual fresh fruit
    tartlets 62
  sweet pizza 82
  see also individual types of
    fruit
fudged espresso shortbread
    112

G

Genoese sponge cake 47
gifts, edible 152–73
glacé fruits: Florentines
    165–7
  Sicilian cassata 122
granita, raspberry 143
grapes: flatbread with grapes
    81
  fig & grape crostata with
    hazelnut crema 66

H

hazelnuts: almond &
    hazelnut amaretti 165
  almond, hazelnut &
    pistachio torrone 157

chestnut, chocolate &
hazelnut cake 17
chocolate & hazelnut
cookies 169
crunchy mini meringues
107
fig & grape crostata with
hazelnut crema 66
Florentines 165–7
hazelnut & carrot cake 16
hazelnut cake 33
sticky plum, hazelnut &
almond tart 54
Tuscan trifle 126
honey: rosemary & orange
honey cake 38–40

I
ice cream: bitter chocolate
ice cream 140
plum ice cream 140
rice ice cream 147
zabaglione ice cream 147
iced drink, vodka lemon 151
ingredients 8
Italian birthday cake 34
Italian croissants 115
Italian doughnuts 92–4
Italian plum cake 47

L
lemon sorbet: vodka lemon
iced drink 151
lemons: blueberry & lemon
drizzle polenta cakes 91
lemon & vanilla cream
pastries 99
lemon & vanilla pastry
cream 103
lemon bread 77
lemon mascarpone
cheesecake 125
raspberry, orange, lemon
& yogurt cake 38
lining tins 8
loaf cakes: cappuccino loaf
cake 44
fragrant coffee &
cinnamon loaf cake 21

M
Marsala wine: zabaglione 134
zabaglione ice cream 147
mascarpone: classic tiramisù
121
lemon mascarpone
cheesecake 125
rice ice cream 147

stuffed figs 134
meringues: crunchy mini
meringues 107
pistachio meringues 158
mombaruzzo, amaretti 161

N O
nuts: chocolate salami 169
oranges: blood orange &
almond cake 29–30
blood orange & Campari
sorbet 148
raspberry, orange, lemon
& yogurt cake 38
rosemary & orange honey
cake 38–40

P
pancakes: the Apostles'
fingers 133
panettone 173
panna cotta 130
pasticciotto 103
pastries: baked sweet
pastries 100
cannoli 96
fried pastry bites 111
lemon & vanilla cream
pastries 99
pasticciotto 103
sweet ricotta pastries 92
pastry cream 62
lemon & vanilla pastry
cream 103
peaches: peach & pistachio
slice 43
peach cremolata 143
pears: chocolate & pear tart
65
pear & almond bread 80
spiced pear & walnut cake
22–4
petit beurre biscuits:
chocolate salami 169
pine nut tart 61
pistachios: almond &
pistachio biscotti 161
almond, hazelnut &
pistachio torrone 157
peach & pistachio slice 43
pistachio cream 158
pistachio meringues 158
rhubarb, rosemary &
pistachio strudel cake 26
pizza, sweet 82
flatbread with grapes 81
plums: Italian plum cake 47
plum ice cream 140

sticky plum, hazelnut &
almond tart 54
polenta: blueberry & lemon
drizzle polenta cakes 91
Prosecco: vodka lemon iced
drink 151
prunes: Umbrian strudel 55

R
raspberries: raspberry granita
143
raspberry, orange, lemon
& yogurt cake 38
rhubarb, rosemary &
pistachio strudel cake 26
rice ice cream 147
ricotta: the Apostles' fingers
133
baked sweet pastries 100
cannoli 96
cherry & ricotta cake 15
fig, amaretti & ricotta tart
73
fig & fennel ricotta bread
78
pine nut tart 61
Sicilian cassata 122
sweet ricotta pastries 92
rosemary: rhubarb, rosemary
& pistachio strudel cake
26
rosemary & orange honey
cake 38–40

S
salami, chocolate 169
savoiardi biscuits: classic
tiramisù 121
semifreddo with caramel figs
144
shortbread, fudged espresso
112
Sicilian cassata 122
sorbet: blood orange &
Campari sorbet 148
lemon sorbet 151
watermelon sorbet 148
spiced fig biscotti 104
spiced pear & walnut cake
22–4
sticky plum, hazelnut &
almond tart 54
strawberries: strawberry
cake 29
strawberry tartlets 58
streusel topping: sweet pizza
82
strudel, Umbrian 55

strudel cake, rhubarb,
rosemary & pistachio 26
stuffed figs 134
sultanas: panettone 173
sweet breads 74–83
fig & fennel ricotta bread 78
flatbread with grapes 81
lemon bread 77
mini cream-filled buns 74
panettone 173
pear & almond bread 80
sweet pizza 82
sweet ricotta pastries 92

T
tarts 48–73
blackberry & chocolate
tart 70
chocolate & pear tart 65
fig, amaretti & ricotta tart 73
fig & grape crostata with
hazelnut crema 66
individual fresh fruit tartlets
62
pine nut tart 61
sticky plum, hazelnut &
almond tart 54
strawberry tartlets 58
Umbrian strudel 55
very berry tart 69
tiramisù, classic 121
torrone, almond, hazelnut &
pistachio 157
trifle: ancient Roman trifle
129
Tuscan trifle 126

U V
Umbrian strudel 55
vanilla: apple vanilla cake
with thick vanilla custard
37
lemon & vanilla cream
pastries 99
lemon & vanilla pastry
cream 103
vodka lemon iced drink 151

W
walnuts: spiced pear &
walnut cake 22–4
watermelon sorbet 148

Y Z
yogurt: raspberry, orange,
lemon & yogurt cake 38
zabaglione 134
zabaglione ice cream 147

ACKNOWLEDGEMENTS

The biggest acknowledgment to Editorial Director, **Julia Charles**, for her tenacity and dedication and for giving me this opportunity again. I am thrilled.

Abi Waters with her wealth of knowledge and expertise and gentle guidance and good humour; shaping this book. The very many errors that you have spotted never making me feel dreadful, joyful to be working with you. Humble thanks and gratitude.

Susan Fleming, my very dear friend of extraordinary talent, we so enjoy our meetings and passionately discussing Italy; and I feel so proud of our collaborations.

Claire Winfield, so peaceful, gentle and totally absorbed in her project. Her extraordinary eye for detail has enriched this book magnificently, *grazie mille*.

Toni Kay, I didn't know it was possible to improve on *Cucina di Amalfi* and *Cucina del Veneto* but I've been proven wrong, wow and double wow. Love your work for the rhythms throughout this book.

Kathy Kordalis, so wonderful to see you and work with you again, such dedication and beautiful cooking and styling – a true artist, full of passion.

To my dear Antonia - from year 6 at school you have always been so actively involved in my career and work and am so incredibly grateful for your interest, support and help.